A
COURSE
IN
CRYSTALS

LESSONS IN PERSONAL TRANSFORMATION
AND
GLOBAL HEALING

ROSE
MORNINGSTAR

1817

Harper & Row, Publishers, San Francisco

New York, Cambridge, Philadelphia, St. Louis
London, Singapore, Sydney, Tokyo

FIRST EDITION

Library of Congress Cataloging-in-Publication Data

Morningstar, Rose.
    A course in crystals.

    1. Crystals — Miscellanea.   I. Title.
BF1999.M7635   1989   133.3'22   88-45676
ISBN 0-06-250601-3 (pbk.)

---

89   90   91   92   93   MCN   .10   9   8   7   6   5   4   3   2   1

To
Leonard W. Ames
and
Una W. Ames

because with their unfailing love,
this life has developed most joyfully

CONTENTS

PART THREE: CRYSTAL LIGHT

PREFACE

When a new book appears on the market, one wonders, sometimes, if all these books are needed. Where are they going? What are they doing? What is their purpose? Communication.

Communication is now more intense than it has ever been. Not only on our little planet, but across the vast universe, communication has revved itself up to a hitherto unknown intensity. Truly, this is a most joyous condition.

So the market is flooded with books, and people are buying them and reading them. In reading *this* book, you will have the opportunity to touch the farthest reaches of yourself. You will be expanding with the universe as you explore together the power of this new and greater form of communication. Move gently. It is a huge, unexplored space; an area that requires great courage and the finest cooperation.

In the journey of creating this book, I have witnessed and experienced this courage and this finer cooperation. It is in this tone, this higher vibration, that I wish to thank Bob Black for his untiring strength and constant cheerful cooperation. I thank Marion McCracken for her insistence that I stay strong and that I "get on with it." I thank Jack and Judith Hogg for their courage and their willingness to search. I thank my editor, Mark Salzwedel, for the inspired, thorough, and sensitive way he handled my manuscript.

And I especially thank my husband, Gordon Ames Hughes, for being my teacher and for standing by me through a transformative experience that tore away the old and thrust us unexpectedly into a new and beautiful beginning.

I love you all, and I Thank you.

Rose Morningstar

INTRODUCTION

Sometimes in the night there are whispers . . . and they ring so true. For days I have been searching for them. In my greater knowing, I have known them. And at night, in the state of sleep, I am free to wander and explore, search about for the answers. Free from my body, I bring the answers back, in whispers. This wandering is a great source. It works beautifully. I have so many more answers than I used to. I know more, undestand more, am kinder and more giving. I am more patient, too. I understand what is meant by "the Great Way is not difficult for those who have no preferences."

Three Augusts ago I went for a weekend retreat to the wilderness. There was a spot I especially liked, in a valley between two steep hills. Nearby, a little stream sifted through mossy stones. Someone had made a little altar, a fire pit, and set two benches on each side. I sat here with my two companions. We sat in quiet stillness for a long time. Then, rather suddenly, the hillside became full of beings. Row upon row of them filled the hill to the south. There were men, women, and children; they came in families. Some moved forward, three came very close. Others stayed back to observe. They were space people. I have no memory of what went on, because I went into a variation of perception to assist them in talking to my two companions. It is somewhat frustrating at times to have so much said and not be there to hear it. But I said that I would be interpreter and voice this time, and I have been true to my promise. When I returned, the bank to the north was full of Native Americans, standing in tiers. They had come to greet the visitors, to observe and to approve, to stand at our sides, to join us in strength.

I was told that our visitors had spoken of many things to come, that they had been observing and working near us for some time, and now was the time for them to reveal themselves and come a bit closer. They requested that I transcribe this primer for them. I was glad that they asked, and agreed readily. It has been a great schooling for me.

Now it is January, Friday the thirteenth. I sit facing south. At high noon, it is seven degrees above zero. Deep snow covers the lawn from this house to the neighbor's. A few dry, yellow leaves cling uncertainly to the bare branches of the maple. Here in the meditation room, the library, it is quiet. I have shut the door from the noise of the secretary and the businessman, my husband, working in the other part of the house. I am in a world of my own. The sun doesn't shine here in this part of the world. Last year, a sum total of thirty-three days was the sun's gift to this area. There is a constant cloud cover from the lake . . . a little depression, a valley of water . . . above and below. I am aware that there are great changes planned for this part of the globe. Galatian spoke of it, and Galatian has been so faithful in the reports, so true to the mark, that I believe it. There are other knowings in me, too . . . simply from myself. Not everything has come from Galatian. I, too, am a source, and there are things that I know.

Galatian is a greater being than the space people we met on the hill. Galatian also includes the Native Americans in flesh that were on the north hill. Galatian includes many who in their greater knowing work to bring the world into a new consciousness. Galatian may include you. You will know after reading this book. For some of us have come to work in a certain pattern in relationship to one another. We have come to forfeit our own rights for those of the group, and we have come to serve. In this serving we will discover ourselves, and we will move with the Earth as she moves into her higher consciousness. We will serve and learn . . . and we will grow.

This book is for you. It is a text of sorts, a primer. It bends its will to your will, for it is only an instrument of instruction. Far be it from us to say we know the whole thing. You have your knowing that fits with our knowing, and together we will become whole.

This primer speaks of crystals from beginning to end. It is written for those who are to work with crystals. Those who made this commitment will find it helpful and interesting. Others will find it of no use. When it falls into your hands, know it is for you.

This book is a dynamic representation of what might ensue if you were to follow a course of events that would lead you to a clearer understanding of crystals. Step by step, you are led through a series of constructed circumstances that represent the changes potentially inherent in crystal utilization. If you were to look at a quartz crystal, one dug from the ground, you would not realize the potential power hidden there. This book, *A Course in Crystals*, makes it clear that we see with very limited vision at this time. Through a series of exercises and disciplines we might bring ourselves — indeed, we are being called to come — to a place of understanding where application of these qualities will benefit the Earth and her populace mightily.

In this process, we will raise ourselves in consciousness, expand our vision, until we see more clearly the interconnectedness of all life forces, both earthly and universal. This book gives you the opportunity to search out the uniqueness of your own character, to relate it to the specific qualities of a particular crystal, and to move forward from there with the development of a complex set of rules that govern these qualities. Hence will come the ability to deduce what benefits to humankind might come from this interaction.

Much of the book works through a process of clarifying your own thought system. Examples are given that set you to thinking about the possibilities of going beyond thought to a space where an expansive memory takes over. Lessons are set up whereby you may work within the confines of your own heart, memorizing phrases, poems, or the affirmations at the end of each lesson, which assist in the process of sensitizing you to an inner knowing that will connect each individual crystal to a planetary grid. This in turn has the potential of forming a network that will enliven the Earth with a new energy system.

The system that has been set up by our higher knowing is beyond our current comprehension. This book is designed to get us more thoroughly in touch with that higher knowing. It is designed to project that which we now know onto a larger screen, to help us realize the enormous potential of our creator selves. In this realization, we will apply new principles we have learned and lift ourselves into a new way of life that is not earthbound, but universal in scope. As you read the book, practice the lessons, exercise your will to create, you build a New Earth where utilization of crystalline energy will not only be possible, but will be necessary. Therefore the training that you will find in this book, which prepares you to handle the higher energies that are universal in nature, is essential. The affirmations at the end of each lesson will lift you into a position of readiness for these higher energies. You will learn to assist in raising the consciousness of the planet and to place crystals in their proper position of usefulness.

In *A Course in Crystals*, it is noted that humankind has not yet reached the ethical purity required to be trustworthy in handling such high energy sources. This book is an attempt to give you a program that will clarify the mind and purify the heart. Thus the way might be cleared for quartz crystals to be brought forth as the major source of energy on this planet. The result will be to change the structure of the planet itself, lifting it into the Light, where the development of all species on it will reflect more fully the nature of God, the universal principle of oneness.

PART ONE

The Hidden Jewel

Lesson 1

THE SPACE CONTINGENT

Yes, dear co-worker, it is we who share this story with you. We have come from afar, and we do bring you jewels of information, for we have set up our laboratory some time ago, and we have much to share.

We unite to form a union with you to help protect, instruct, and to teach-learn *with* you about these fractals, these crystal pyramids of light and living, these machines that echo the universe in their completeness.

We work with others. We are a unit of many. Some are earthbound and in spirit—largely Native American in nature. Some are earthbound and in flesh. Some are angelic in nature and have never been earthbound, but simply work with the higher forces in service to the earth. Some of us are as those called people from space. We have traveled far to come do this work. It is an assignment we have given ourselves and is of long standing. We have learned much in the last three hundred years and are ready to share it. We are anxious to begin, because we have not yet worked with the crystals in conjuction with exploration on the Earth's surface. We have only pulled their energy into our realms to explore it and learn to work with it. Now we are anxious to see what it will do in conjunction with the Earth forces.

Those of us who call ourselves Galatian are a unit, yet we can be divided into many parts. We join to assist one another in this work. We come from many schools of learning to bring our skills and understanding, to meld them into a working unit whose proper function is to bring peace to Earth. As in old, wise men brought gifts to the Babe, so we too bring jewels of precious value to the Christ consciousness, to the uplifted heart and mind, and we bear them for the sake of peace on Earth and good will to all. Precious jewels formed by the Earth herself are now ready to provide their services and we must, like the wise men, bring them to the Christ child—the consciousness of Christ within—and provide them a means for their service. These jewels of the Earth are brought to serve the Earth, and we are the implements of devotion. Devoted to the prospect of the Christ consciousness in everyone, filling the Earth with light, we work with these fractals of light and living, these crystals, knowing that they have the potential to generate much activity that will assist us in our task.

We come now to join you and to dictate this story, this primer, that we might all more fully understand one another and work in more open harmony. You too are a unit in Galatian, those of you who dwell in Earth. Those of you who have committed yourselves to working with crystals are a unit in the Galatian source and are bound to be most active on the Earth plane. We need you to assist us, else we could not implement our task into the third dimension. Someone has to be there also, you understand, to hold the energy, to receive the information. To work in conjunction with the rest of the units in Galatian is your chosen task, and we are glad to communicate more openly with you, largely due to the fact that we now have a scribe. Communication is sometimes difficult between the several layers of dimensions. Vibrations come haltingly when they are transposed from one frequency to another. We are fortunate when we have a channel who can speak in both vibrations at once and reach out into the different levels to help us communicate. Our scribe will let us know from time to time when a new publication is needed, and we will oblige by sending the proper information through for the necessary training for the moment.

It is a work-and-learn-as-you-go situation for all of us . . . for none of us have been here before. We are coming back, yes, we have been on Atlantis and worked in many other places as well with jewels akin to those we now approach. There is a difference, however. These are purer, of higher quality and more refined. None of us have ever been *here* before.

"The space contingent is essential to what we humans are and what we are to be."

Lesson 2

FRACTALS OF LIGHT

The physical body is an instrument of devotion and service. Brought into being by thought, it supplements the actions being carried out in other spheres. It is composed of fractals of light. A fractal is a unit of energy that has no comparison smaller than its size. It represents the form for which it exists. It exists for the greater being of which it is a part. For example, you are a fractal of Galatian. If you work with crystals, you are. Together we make the whole unit of crystal workers. We are fractals of the same form.

In speaking of fractals, we must mention the living pyramids of light. Functioning in every prism of light is a pyramid of energy. This energy forms a pattern that is universal. When we say universal, we do not mean it is somehow vaguely represented here and there, spaced in appropriate portions of the universe . . . no . . . think smaller.

Take the tip of your thumb. How does it replace itself constantly? The wear and tear it experiences requires ever-moving flows of energy to keep your thumb a thumb and not a finer density experience of nothingness. Built in microscopic pyramid shapes, it constantly maintains centers of energy that adhere to each other to continue a specific density relationship, else there would be no thumb.

Now what enables this existence? Brought from the finer ethers into the third dimension for practical use, it originates and is maintained by thought. It must constantly maintain itself at one level or rate of speed. Pryamid energy is a very controllable, manipulable form of energy. Placed side by side, each unit, or center of energy, rotates in its own beingness and yet at the same time coexists or exists within bordering energy. Now how can we say "coexists or exists within" another energy? The phraseology depends on how large a pyramid you are drawing or encompassing. For if every center of energy existing in the universe forms itself in pyramid shape, then the shape can take whatever size it desires or needs.

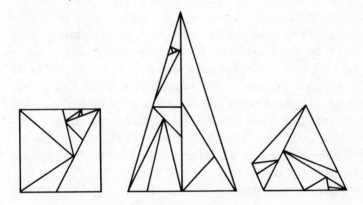

Draw a shape with straight lines, any shape. Break it into triangles with other straight lines. It can always be done. No straightlined object is outside of the pyramid law on a flat surface or in the second dimension. Carry this law up into the third dimension and through every other dimension, and there is no escaping it. All centers of energy are pyramidal in nature. Large or small, it doesn't matter.

Now, when you construct a pattern of crystal energy, it is good to understand this law, for measurements and controls are necessary. Borders and separations are necessary. Understanding the unit measures of the pyramid, seeing it within the object, learning to watch it function, beginning to understand it, are prerequisites for working with crystal energy. To control it is all important, for it is powerful. It is the energy of the universe tapped. It can best be controlled with the mind.

Study the tip of your thumb again. Produce in your thumb health . . . with a thought, produce it. This is pyramids responding to your thought. This is energy moving in the form of pyramids energized by your mind. This is mind control. Your mind is powerful when it understands. Begin to see in pyramids . . . everything. It is training for your work with crystals.

The visual measurements will fade away when they need to, so that you can work with the denser reality. Have no fear that the abstraction will overtake you, for it is no abstraction at all. It is the basis of reality on *all* dimensions and can be seen, through your eye, in the third dimension to help you understand the power you work with—indeed *must* be seen if you are to do your work. So practice, practice seeing things in pyramids. Follow that energy. Become sensitive to it. You will begin to understand what you are to do and how you are to do it. Move in this energy. Comprehend it. The mind will explore and expand, and new insights will come that will lay a solid groundwork for the project. Live with it. It will come.

When we approach the high energy of a crystal, when we attempt to set it in motion, we must realize with what energy we are working. We have called it the energy of the universe tapped. Embedded in a crystal of any size is a complete energy. All the spectrums of the universal force are crystallized here. When one draws on a partial force, one sees a limited amount of energy. When one draws on a full force, one is dealing with unlimited energy. A crystal is unlimited energy. Able to constantly renew itself, able to draw continual nourishment from the cosmic energy of the universe, a crystal never tires and never depletes itself. To harness this energy with good intent is one of the jobs of many of us who labor to bring in the New Age.

If some of this material seems elementary, bear with it. In learning to manipulate powerful energy, we begin with the basics. We don't skip them just because our egos are impatient.

We do well to hold the ego by the scruff of the neck and say, "You're important to me, yes, but let's get one thing straight: I'm in charge here, this higher self of me wants to produce for humankind. You might lend me your assistance, but remember, I'm in charge."

In working with crystals, there are those of us who are exposed to the Earth plane. We are nearby, and we desire to work closely with you who are grounded on the planet. To flow the crystalline energy heavenward is one thing, to flow it into the bowels of the Earth is another. All precautions must be taken to control and to learn to use this power with great respect. For centuries now, those of us who work with crystals from our position in space have been drawing the energy upward, learning with it, and experiencing the benefits of it. Now the time has come for us to share with you our knowledge and experience. We are ready to share if you are willing.

As we have worked with your crystals — for *yours* they are — over the last few years, we have discovered several things. One is that the energy drawn flows easily upward, that is, away from the center of the planet. But it is with great difficulty that it flows parallel to the planet center, and with even more resistance in the movement as it attempts to flow *toward* the planet center. This fact should give you some idea as to how important it is to begin to see in pyramids and understand the energy flow contained in them. For when energy varies its speed, the greatest concentration of the mind has to be held and controlled in order to use this energy correctly and to get it to do one's bidding. Let loose without controls, it has the capacity to destroy things we might not want destroyed, and it also has the capacity to construct things we might not want to bring into the new planet, the New Earth.

So watch the containment of your controls from this moment on. Watch how you control yourself, your emotions, your thoughts, your willingness to do things or not to do things. It is this control of self that you must master if you are to be a guiding force for crystals. Do you remember Mr. Spock in "Star Trek"?

He was part way there. He depicted one who was on his way to learning self-control of the kind we mention. Don't take him as a role model, but realize, please, that this concept of mind control is not foreign to your planet. The Great Buddha called it nonattachment. You will do well to develop it, if you are to fulfill your work with crystals. Most of you who previously made this commitment are well into establishing abilities in this area.

Try visualizing a pyramid of light. See it rotate clockwise at its energy center, and bring this rotating energy slowly to the surface of the prism. Allow it to rotate on the surface. See it in rainbow colors, for it *is* full spectrum. Rotate it in your mind's eye around the surface of the pyramid. Watch it. Now pull it back into the center, condense it, pull it together, make it smaller without subtracting from its content. Now rotate it clockwise as a knot, a bead in the center of the structure. The edges of the structure

are now empty of energy. You have contained it, you have concentrated it in the center of the pyramid, and you are rotating it clockwise. *You* are rotating it. Slowly bring it to rest. Let it just sit, sparkling with energy, alive with potential, let it just sit. Now slowly, ever so slowly, begin to rotate it counterclockwise. Bring it slowly into action and slowly, slowly expand it. Don't let it get out of your control. Contain it . . . and expand it. Counterclockwise it goes. It enlarges, *you* allow it to enlarge. It enlarges only as much as you say it can. As you control it, it moves toward the periphery of the pyramid. Watch it. Allow it to go only to the edge and no farther. Keep it going in the counterclockwise flow. Move it. Now slowly center it again. Bring it back into the center. Condense it. Slowly, ever so slowly, still it. Bring it to rest. Let it center itself and be still. Throw your own protective energy around it. Bless it. Put it to rest. Turn your back on it . . . but only after you have seen it still and safe.

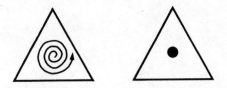

Now we will instruct you. Moving in a clockwise motion this energy builds, creates. Moving in a counterclockwise position, this energy destroys, tears apart. It is powerful. Even in your mind it is powerful. We caution you. Lift your heart in love, for to work with crystals in any other form of attitude destroys the purpose for which we have come to you. We come in love to assist in the building of the New Earth. We come in love. Meet us in love, and we will work well together. We are a powerful force. Together we form a great union. We have work to do, if *you* will it. We are glad in our hearts we have come. We hope you are, too.

⬦⬦⬦⬦⬦

"Fractals of Light glimmer within; we accept and increase them."

Lesson 3

PYRAMID POWER

We will now speak of pyramid power, concentrating on the power aspect of the beingness of this form of energy. Are there other forms of energy? Yes, there are many ways of looking at the same thing. From one angle, an object might look round, from another it might look flat. From still another, convex or oblique. However one might think of it as all one energy, still one must admit that the uses are so varied and multifaceted that it becomes varied enough in nature to be treated as different energies. Here we concentrate on pyramid energy for the benefit of our working with crystals.

If you will move along inside of a crystal, you will discover many things. First, let us draw the crystal. What colors shall we make it? Let's start with blue. Let's make it cobalt blue. The whole of it rather dense in color and cobalt from one end to the other, equally colored in all parts. Yet, let's look closer. It is a crystal, remember, so in its depths is the rainbow, the ever-present rainbow. There is never a crystal without it in its entirety.

From one surface to the other, from one end to the other, it is rainbow, yet it is cobalt at the same time in its entirety. Commingling, coexisting, two aspects, two functions within the same beingness. The cobalt is the effects of eons of labor. Pressed hard to the mother's breast, this energy nourished itself and nourished itself, drawing from the Earth the needed supplies to form itself and crystallize its energy into the form of helpfulness it now is. Ready to release its power, ready to let its stored battery be sprung, it sits and waits for activation.

Now, what will it produce? Let's explore its inner workings, its shape, size, and makeup. Its breadth is about eighteen inches and its length about four feet. Starting at the base, we will see a rough line of surface, craggy in nature, blunt and faceted in such manner that it does not reflect much light. This is where she drew her nourishment, and this is where she broke away from that nourishment when she was completed and perfect for functioning. Moving up the side we see the folds of energy flattened, smooth and reflecting much light; at the top we see a peak as that of a blunt pencil.

Stand back a moment and look at her. There she lies. You have just unearthed her. Coming with sacred tools, blessed in the sun, you and your carefully chosen companions, four in number, making five in all, have unearthed her. And she lies, for the first time in centuries, in the sun. Dappled by the falling shadows of leaves (for it was in the deep woods you found her) she lies motionless, yet there is an aliveness about her, an energy that is concentrated and powerful. As you smoothed the damp soil from her, once you had surfaced her, as you rubbed her clean, you felt this concentration as if there were more than material here, indeed it seemed like life, living power.

Entering through the craggy bottom we can explore and find that there is a heavy chakra beginning about three inches up and centering about six inches into her stem. It is light in nature, composed of light, yet it is heavy because it beats at a rhythm slower paced than her higher centers. Moving beyond this and upward, we explore to find the next centering of energy flow, more rapid in beat and more fluid in motion. She is a five-chakra crystal, and she resonates in each center as if she has just been discovered. She matches your five upper chakras. There is faint music in your ears. In your own centers, matching hers, you feel the pull, the drawing, the matching of energies.

THE CHAKRA CENTERS

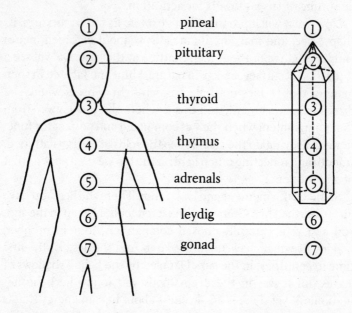

At her crown is a pinpoint of energy, a ray going forth at an eighty-two-degree angle, where a beam of light, caught correctly, can be seen. This is the greatest emission of power, the greatest concentration. Here one must watch to not be damaged, to not misuse, here is the potential for great works. Here is the need to learn manipulation and control, great mind control.

Now what of the deep blue nature, the cobalt blue? Draw back a moment and look at the hills about you. Rise off your own knoll, lift yourself above the trees, and look about. Over there is buried a smoky crystal, over there a golden one, beyond that a very long clear one. You placed them here, you deposited them here, long ago, and they wait with their many and varied abilities for you to raise yourself to the level where you can meet yourself full force and work with them. There are many, hill beyond hill, beyond hill . . . and they wait.

To find them before you are ready is impossible, so don't try. They would disappear from the planet before they would yield to your uncleanness, so prepare. Prepare yourself for your service. Cleanse from yourself all hate, all avarice, and all greed. Stand before your Creator as an implement of service and of love. Those of you who cleanse first will be the first to work with and touch the stones. Yield yourself to cleansing. Work at it. It takes courage and determination. Serene in your attempt, move forward with the strength of a steel blade. Don't be affected by those who would deter you. Keeping a heart full of compassion, move forward with strength. Use every discipline necessary to get you there. You will make it. Proceed step by step. Know yourself. Better yourself. Correct your actions, control them, and you will see the day when the crystal light will reflect on your face, and all humankind will benefit from it.

◇◆◇◆◇◆◇

"Pyramid power builds; we lend our minds and build with it."

THE CRYSTAL ENLIGHTENMENT

In the movements of times to come, you will see much use of the crystals. In an enlightened age, we make use of our highest resources. In an unenlightened age, we are blind to the potential about us. We are moving from an unenlightened age. We have started on this age of enlightenment rather abruptly. We would do well to recognize the speed with which it comes upon us and prepare ourselves rapidly. With this in mind, let us return to our cobalt blue crystal and become more acquainted with it.

Lying here in the dappled sunlight, our crystal has been carefully rubbed clean and given a warm nest of fresh, sweet earth, free of stones or any hard objects. It lies in a soft bed of moisture and richness free of obstructions. In this way, its energy can center and flow freely, it can adjust to its new environment. It can rouse and shake itself a little bit and adapt to the openness, the open field of conductivity it is now experiencing. Let it center. Touch it infrequently. Allow it time to center and adjust. Watch the air around it. There is a glow, if you will perceive it. Entering into this glow, you feel an aliveness on the surface of your skin. Touching the aura of the glow, the most outward extended part, you feel pressure, warmth, and fine movement on the palms of your hands.

Walk around the blue stone. Study it. It will perceive you as you perceive it. So if you wish to work with it, hold your thoughts high and your intentions pure. Have you heard of the automatic cutoff? Have you experienced governors? Those devices that control power operate here also. Built into every crystal that was planted is an automatic cutoff, a device that will shut the power down completely, if it is to be used in willfulness and wrong-doing. It is simple in structure. The energy of a pure crystal brought from Atlantis in love at the time of the clearing has within it such purity, such a high calling, such high vibrations that when it is attempted to feed these vibrations to the elements of evil or wrongdoing, they automatically cut off . . . for can you feed a higher-energy current through a lower-energy circuit . . . without burning it out?

So now, those who would use the crystal machine as an object of derision, those who do not respect its quality, its pureness, and its high calling had better beware. For not only do they risk their own sacredness, but they force energy to contain itself within them and their efforts will come to naught. It will end in disaster. For these crystals were not sent for selfishness, they were sent in love for the fine, high calling of the implementation of a new age. Beware those who would use them otherwise. Much precious time could be wasted, for it is *now* that we need our flowering and soon will come our fruiting. For the time is at hand when all people will bow to one another in respect. Honoring one another in due course, as the movements of the Earth flow into the lessons, the corrections, and the changes that come, humankind will come to understand the need for oneness. The network will be formed wherein we will be a blessing to one another and enhance one anothers' greatness, correcting one anothers' faults.

We will follow now the course of events surrounding the crystal as you move into working with it. It wishes to do some work. How are you to cooperate with it to bring it to its greatest potential? First of all, treat it with great respect. Not in the worshipful sense, but in the way that one might respect a very powerful coworker. Know full well that the coworker has the ability to control the job, but if the correct goals are to be obtained, effort must be made to cooperate fully and equally, each one subduing personal power to the all.

How do you determine how a crystal must sit to work with the greatest efficiency? Behold how much you will learn as you work. Your sensitiveness must come to the point of abstraction, if you are to understand the divine elements in the crystal in order to work with it knowledgeably. Reach inside the crystal now with your mind. Use your greatest mind, and reach inside. What do you see? Follow that line from the root chakra, explore with your vision and your heart sense, and see what you find. Close your eyes now. Sit back in your chair. What do you see?

⬦⬦⬦⬦

"The crystal enlightenment comes forth; we will it to be."

Lesson 5

THE BLUE CRYSTAL

We have trudged the hill. We have exposed the deep blue crystal. We have blessed it in the sun. We have carefully cleansed it. We have made it a bed of soft, moist soil. We have helped purify ourselves by our dedication and our love. We have held our palms to the sun and stated that our hearts are clean, our intent pure. We have given the thanksgiving ceremony for this duty, this blessing. Now what are we to do?

Understand the crystal. Understand your own individual crystal. Each one is different. Each one has been empowered in a unique way. Each has its own personality, its own functions and duty. Each was perfected for a certain task.

Now what of this cobalt blue crystal, here in our gaze, at our feet? Have you searched it with your mind? Have you explored its innards until you begin to get a feel of what's in there? Have you touched with your mind, your inner eye, the might contained here . . . the magic? Do you follow its trace to its highest chakra? Know it well, with feeling. Not something you could write in a book or an instruction pamphlet, but a knowing in the heart, an understanding in the mind that can be *known* but not spoken. There are no words to speak such.

When you know your crystal this well, when you live on the inside of it as well as the outside, then is the time to right it. We caution you: Do not right it until you know it. You will only have to lay it down again and begin from the start once more if you right it too soon. For only in the knowing of the balance of your crystal will you right it correctly. Be patient, be correct and accurate. You will know when you know your crystal. It may take a year or more of studying and close association, much meditation in closeness. You will know when you know. If you don't know, you don't know.

In righting the crystal, you ask of it which side it wishes to face north and which side must face south. You ask which end down, which up? You ask the angle. Does the point of contact with the earth force slant up the hill or down? What setting or structure do we frame it in? Must this structure hold elements of gold, or will copper suffice? What is the cost of this structure? Who will frame it? Who meld it? Whom can we trust? Who wishes to do this service in understanding and purity? How does it adhere to the ground, how bedded? Where does the point of contact of the crystal to the standing structure come in? Where must they touch? Where must they *not* touch? How far must the crystal be lifted from the ground to bring out its greatest potential? What is its potential? What use, this crystal?

These questions you answer with your inner knowing. These questions you answer in meditation. Meditation is no longer a time apart. Meditation is now your inner knowing and it is done on your feet, in your heart, as you work. As you get to know your crystal, many great understandings come to you involving your own greatness and your own potential. Clearer understanding comes to you about why you entered the planet Earth this time, why you are here, what you promised to do. As these developments take place inside you, you grow in knowledge of your crystal and you begin to see the whole thing coming together. Your reason for being here, your training so far, all begin to make sense. You see a pattern unseen before. The design in the universe becomes a little more personal. You feel you belong more than ever before. It all begins to make sense.

Let us speak again about fractals, the pyramids of light and living. Condensed once more into the world of fractals, we can explore the inner workings of our crystal. We will continue to develop on the cobalt blue crystal, for it has the qualities and capacities of most, yet dwells in its uniqueness.

We have now righted our crystal. We have found the meldor, have blessed him or her with our work. Not once did the meldor see the crystal while building the frame, and this was some frustration, yet he or she built it correctly to our specifications and instructions. We assured the meldor that someday he or she would see the object for which the frame was built, but for the present it must be kept a secret. The meldor thought of it as some trade secret—which indeed it is, in a new sort of way. For we trade good for evil, and we shall continue in this bartering and trading till naught is left but good.

Our crystal stands there, her frame affixed to the ground. This one is neither male or female, for she is *both*, and either pronoun is correct. Sometimes the function will be male and one will sense to call him masculine. Sometimes the function will be feminine, and this gender will be sensed and fall from the lips. She functions in her fullness. Both negative and positive rotate within her. There are those crystals that will be fully masculine in nature, and they will have counterpart crystals, sometimes at great distances. With these counterpart crystals, they will draw and pull energy, receiving it and returning it, and the one with the feminine nature will receive, replenish, and return in kind. Many units will be empowered in betwixt the two crystals as the energy passes through them. Many miles will be empowered.

However, here in our blue crystal we have both genders, and we deal with a complete unit ready to do its service in the immediate area. Generating energy that can be felt for miles around, it now sits with its inner eyes twinkling, waiting for us to understand it. It is a mystery yet. It sits like a jewel in its gold-worked frame. It is stable, firmly placed, and at most times covered from view. It tolerates this cover, for it knows that the time has not yet come for its total exposure. There will be the day of surrounding gardens when the oleander, wisteria, and rhododendron

in abundance will be about it, but now is the time for quietness.
The day for visitors has not yet come.

This is the time for learning the machine, and she is surrounded at this time with boards for sitting, ropes and canvas for covering, and a hut nearby where the guardians in flesh bide their time in watching and caring. She is a working implement, and she is beauty beheld. A bit staggering to behold, for her beauty holds such machinery . . . and we are beginning to see it. In the etheric—that part of reality that builds in spirit before it becomes physical—the cogs move, the wheels spin, and we begin to see them. We bring them into the third dimension with our eyesight, and we begin to comprehend what is going on. We also begin to comprehend our coworkers more fully. Feeling them brush by us in our work, we now begin to see them. Our eyes, our minds are beginning to reach successfully into the fourth and fifth dimensions.

While we attended her at night, we began to hear her song. And rising in altered sleep, we saw the stars surrounding her and we sensed the movement of the energy gears and saw too the forms moving about tending and honing her, bringing her to a crisp perfection after her long sleep. So now, even in the sunlight, we begin to see more clearly and sense those about us working with us. We begin to communicate with them, and it is a great help. For some of them have, more recently than us, been working with her and many other crystals.

◇◇◇◇◇

"Rainbow crystals dance joyfully in our day; we see them clearly."

ONENESS IN LIGHT

Do you begin to see the working unit as it flows from one sphere to another? Do you now begin to feel a part of the oneness that has come together to impart valuable information and to assist in the work with crystals? Realize the expansion of the subject. Know that it moves into many Earth realms. There are many facets to this work; it will cover much territory in its assistance to humankind. It will take many avenues. It is a subject for much thought and study. The practical applications are far-reaching.

We will build systems of energy from one coast to another, and they will be empowered by crystals. It will be the new Atlantis. It will be the third dimension brought into Christ consciousness. What does it mean, this Christ consciousness understanding? Exactly what does it mean?

There once was a man who walked the Earth who was the embodiment of love. He worked at it. A soul bound for heaven, as in the old hymns, he walked the Earth many times in many phases of established energy patterns to learn love. As Indian, as ruler, as priest, as peasant, as male, as female, many times he came to learn this passage of love. There were many like him learning this process of love, learning kindness to others. For love is naught but kindness.

They formed a unit too. They became the unit of the Christ consciousness. Holding the Light to the Earth plane, they persisted in their closeness to Earth until the Earth caught fire with the meaning, with the understanding of love. They still persist, and we call their pressure the coming of the Christ consciousness.

Lit in every man and woman is a fire. In the jeweled center of every soul is this light. From it radiates the being. A beautiful creation it is, this soul. It is an instrument of creativity. It is an instrument that is a fractal of God, the great Creator, the original creator, the only creator there is, the whole being. You are a fractal of that being. You *are* that being. Your consciousness, when it becomes a group consciousness, moves to become the Christ consciousness. Opening up to one another, we learn kindness, we learn giving, sharing, and responding with love.

Now where does all this take us? It leads us to understand the greatest creation we have ever made. It leads us to the Christ consciousness of the Earth plane. When a planet brings itself to the point of completion, then it must transpose its energy from one form to another. Our planet Earth has reached this point. She is transposing her energy from one dimension to another. She is lifting her face to the sun, exposing it, and taking a giant step forward. It is a birth, a rebirth, an experience that takes due process and must follow the laws. All processes are governed by universal laws, and this process, this birth of the Earth into greater realms, is no exception. Each law must be followed, and some of those souls who do not move with the Earth into a higher consciousness will be left behind to build their own earth. They are not doomed. They are simply left behind to build their own new earth. It will be of their own making, and they will build a structure that will suit them in their learning.

As for us, those of us who choose to move on with the New Earth and her new consciousness must also build our new space. It is a parturition process, a birthing, and in birth there is always separation. The old must be separated from the new, and those of us who work with the new consciousness must leave the old behind. We must build anew using new tools, new understandings, and new energy.

Now you say there is no such thing as new energy in the

universe. True. Yet there is a freshness to this process of using energy that makes it new. These fractals of energy, these crystals that copy the universe in their completeness are new. Even to themselves they are new. For never have *they* been here before. This is what creation is. Taking something from the old, rearranging it, and making something new. Now what is the new life here? When you breathe into something, you give it new life. When you construct something that has never been constructed before, you create. We are cocreators. And the whole unit, the entire thing, this is the created or the creator. It is one and the same. For in God's likeness we are created, and in this likeness do we create as we build the new world. God is love. It is this simple.

❖❖❖❖❖

"All is well; we move toward oneness in Light."

Lesson 7

THE NATURAL PLACES

There are many places on this planet Earth that are unusually beautiful. High peaks of mountains, caves beneath the ground, areas where wind, rivers, or oceans of long ago have carved structures of stone so overwhelming to the eye that they are instantly inspirational. Each of you knows of certain, special places like this. Marked by nature, they become special. Some have been faithfully preserved. Many lie in wait for the day they will be restored to their natural beauty and their original sacred use. They are not just a few; they are more than a handful. In every county there might be one such area, and to a greater or lesser degree, depending on size and use, they will nourish the area in which they exist.

We have spoken of the gardens that will some day surround the crystals of light and living. In such places as these, the natural places, will abide many crystals. Chosen well for their specific functions, they will be transplanted in these areas of healing and enlightenment, and there will be many gardens, large and small, for us to work in. You have heard of the original garden, you have dreamed stories of it as a child, now is your opportunity to build it on the planet of your choice, your love, your Earth mother, the one who has nourished you many times to your completion. Does it seem too great a fantasy to you? Dare you dream of a world full of love and beauty? My dear co-worker, dream. Know that it is the potential, and know that it is what we work for . . . and we would not work for it if it were not possible.

Envision an Earth full of love. Envision an Earth where there is no ugliness. Envision an Earth that is heaven brought home. Now is the time that has been spoken of for eons, in every climate . . . over the whole globe. In every culture there have been dreams. Now is the time of birthing, of flowering, fruiting, and harvesting. *Now* is the time. Our Earth has come to her fullness. She is ripe for repair. The cleansing is in process and she is to come into her own as a new being, one made whole and alive with a new life. The transposition will take place as we work on it. It is a fact, a reality. We must shape it as we see fit, for it is our creation. Built on love, it will form before us as we move in our new knowing, our new comprehension of what is to be.

Operating always in kindness and consideration for our fellow beings, we move step by step toward our goal of completion of the process. Encouraged in our work by our vision, our knowledge of the Earth-made-whole, we work with patience and firmness when we are faced with those who would obstruct us; and we work with free-flowing, explosive energy when there is no obstruction. Faced with tasks that are not always pleasant, we explore the possible alternatives and move with faith. Keeping cheerful against great odds at times, we gain strength as we learn to handle adversity with courage and determination.

There will be challenges. Doubt not that there will be great need at times for union and assisting one another, as we work our way through what is called the cleansing period. It is, in truth, a separating process, a period of parturition, wherein the old is cast aside from the new, so the new can form its own identity separate from the old. It is not as if debris is being cast off. It is, more clearly, one being separating itself from another so that both might continue in their lives unencumbered by one another, since they have different paths, different destinies to fulfill. This is the birth of the New Earth from the old.

If this New Earth is to be a garden of beauty, we must hold in our hearts the knowledge that this is possible. All doubt must be put aside, for in doubting we destroy. We tear down our own creations, making our work much more difficult. Each time we doubt, we plant tiny seeds that sprout the wrong kind of energy. We build up resistance to the creative vibration when we allow ourselves to feel that all this is not possible, that it is a wild dream, a fantasy.

It is with our minds that we build. Your mind builds or destroys what it wishes. Learn to discipline your mind. Learn to control it. Let it not linger on things you do not wish to happen. Allow it not to dwell on things you do not want to build. Mind is the builder. And *your* mind builds what *you* think. It creates what you create with it. As we move into the New Age, as we grow into and live in this higher vibration, the strength of this law will become more apparent. We will learn to watch our thoughts carefully, for we will find that an undisciplined mind causes much havoc and the eventual effect of it falls back onto the original creator, the one who originated the first uncooperative thought.

So watch for the natural places as you move about. Determine in them what kind of garden you would like to see restored there. Know that from these seeds planted in our minds, we will now grow great gardens. Share your dreams with others. Travel from place to place, and share what you have seen. If you have seen a vision, if you have peeked into the future, and you have seen a natural bridge, for example, a great garden, acres and acres restored to their natural beauty, commercialism gone, say so. Share this vision and enliven other minds with it. Notice as you travel that there is a change in the pallor of the land. Faint with exhaustion she is, yes, but there is a new rosiness rising here and there about the land, new colors, new liveliness, new hope. It is still weak, and one must sometimes search for it, but it can be seen. We are beginning to come into our own again as lovers of the Earth. We are beginning to see once again our duty and how we fit in with the natural cycle of evolution. We are beginning to see our responsibilities to the balance of the all.

⬦⬦⬦⬦⬦

"The natural places call; we answer and attend."

THE HEALING CENTER

Shall we return once again to our blue crystal? How is it progressing? No longer hidden from view, it begins to form around itself the atmosphere of a garden. More people have been added to those who attend it. An around-the-clock vigil is kept in meditation. Different souls offering their service and their understanding have been screened, and there are those who have stayed on to work at close hand and to perpetuate the vigil.

It is a process of centering energy, allowing it to flow where it will, yet tracking it down, centering it at one point. A strong contact must be made at a base point, for the energy is to be sent out in colorful ribbons of helpfulness. Having a strong tie-in at one point is essential for the constant flow, the uninterrupted contact. To let it free of the crystal would disconnect it from our control, and this must not happen. So we are now in the process of establishing a strong tie between the crystal and the energy that floats from it, enhanced by the interaction of the human souls accompanying it in a working relationship. Notice that we say *enhanced by*, for the activity of humans in conjunction with the crystal is a necessary part of the whole machine. A crystal by itself would be inept and unable to do the healing. Used in conjunction with the human force of mind, it becomes a great healer, a great generator of powerful energy.

As the garden develops around our crystal, those working with spades and love have carefully transplanted shrubs and brought cuttings ready for the ground. Benches have been placed with sensitivity and delicacy, and an altar shelter has been built for meditation.The ground is kept pure and free from any foreign contamination that might change the chemical disposition of wholeness.

We begin to feel that this area is being readied for a specific purpose. We have envisioned large crystals of different genders that will send productive energy from county to county, crossing many miles. This energy is picked up and reinforced by other large crystals many times, until a vast area is well supplied with useful energy. We have envisioned transportation energized by crystals. We have seen light, heat, movement of water powered by crystal energy.

So what is happening here, with the blue crystal? Alone in the garden, working by itself, unassisted by other crystals, it has a function of its own. Made of the right proportions and properties, its framework holds it aloft, several inches from the ground. It sits as a learning tool and we are learning, as the garden grows around us, to sense its energy, to use it and control it. It is for healing. Singing its own tune in a healing ray, this crystal in this garden is for healing. This crystal will also help physical difficulties, but it specializes in the healing of mental fractures and emotional imbalances. Do not narrow this down in your mind to propose a kind of clinic, for this it is not; it is much more. There are outer buildings being built at the same time as the garden. Domes are practical in this area, and the steep bank is becoming alive with those transporting materials. Careful not to endanger the growth cycle of the displaced wildlife and shrubbery, the one-room cabins are going up out of sight of the crystal and hidden from each other.

To be a healing center for those who work to regain their emotional balance, to be a place of peace and strength giving, this center must choose carefully not only materials and supplies, but also those who work here. For no contaminants are needed in the body, mind, or spirit. We are working with healing and we must first be healed ourselves.

Those who move along the Path are often asked to turn and go back a few paces to help those, whom they love, who have lingered behind. In this process of returning and assisting, we learn the final cleansings for ourselves. As this mountainside center for healing with its powerful blue crystal is being built, those who build it will experience healing, and it will grow into form as a vital thing grows into full usage: rich, potent, and alive with the giving essential of life.

When all people in their hearts harbor naught but love, then the time will have come for rejoicing. Now is the time of work. With joy in our hearts to sustain us, we move forward in the work, for we know that naught shall transpire lest we do it ourselves. There is much work to be done. Beginning with the recreating of the crystal system, we shall move into works that create a new Earth. The crystal system is only the beginning. It is the groundwork. It is the basic structure and must be laid in order to bring the rest through. It must be established first, for much of the other depends on it. If we are to empower a new world, the crystal system must be laid. So let us work on it diligently, moving forward with faith that as we work, we build anew a system that we have known about, yet this time we build more correctly and more completely.

Beginning with the small crystals in hand, we work to understand the larger ones, and we pray fervently that this time we do it in purity. Each occasion of people on the Earth planet is to make amends for those times when we have chosen to cast aside the laws and abide by our own rulings. At this time we have the opportunity to correct a collective indiscretion. As a group, we moved into the incorrectness, now as the same group we will have the opportunity to build anew that which we understand, and we will do it for the benefit of all humankind.

As you work with the small crystals, the ones held in hand, know that they are duplicates of the larger. Work with them in this understanding, and please know that you are being trained to explore the usages of many crystals, large and small. It is a technique of exploration, for we must build as we grow. To create a new world, we must create, and creation is not what it seems. Creation is hard work. It is not just the waving of a hand. It is building step by step that which we wish to see manifested. We are truly co-creators, and we have come into our own. We have now reached the period of development where we may take the raw materials and create. There was a time when we waited and were formed according to the law. No longer. We now take the law into our own hands, and we create with it. It does not create us. We have reached the point of power where we can move either way. We can move with the law and create magnificently, or we can move against the law and create our own structure, which will fall. Choose once again, and this time choose love.

As we worked together in the old days, we will work together once again. The same souls abide in us. We are the same beings. Moving with the same intelligences, we come again to construct our own world. Let us not slip up this time. Let us hold firm to the conviction that as we move in might, we must also move with the right. Effort put forth in this manner can only reap the benefits of the universe. Holding *that which is not to be* far behind us, let us look forward to building a new world that is empowered by Light and sustained by love.

"The healing center builds around us as we heal ourselves within."

DIVINING CHOICES

When it comes to the time of parting, there are many things that must be thought of in relationship to the circumstances and what they might bring if altered. Practical planning has to be done. It is not by magic that we work the works of God, it is by effort put forth in the right direction. Learning direction is an important step in the process of moving toward Christ consciousness. Each decision is a turning point, and one can turn in many directions. The bend must be constantly in the direction of the right . . . the correct action taken for all those concerned . . . the best action possible for the welfare of all. There are many alternatives. Some are more nearly right than others. There is always one most correct decision. There will be many decisions to make. In a time of change, this is always so.

In the old days, and still in some remote areas, the people of the Chinese culture held the jade stone in the left palm to assist them in decision making. This method was used even in the marketplace to help strike the fair and just bargain. Jade was thought to have a calming effect, a cooling effect, and since the energy for deciding has to be drawn from the greater aura — the greater being that dwells outside the flesh — the energy entering through the left hand might pass through the influence of the jade and thus help obtain and sustain a level head.

What would be the effects on you of minerals in your environment? Consider the following: What if you were to make for yourself several beds . . . if you were to take smoothly polished stones, all of an even size, and make several beds? Build the wood frames in your mind: Make them four inches high, well over six feet in length, and wide enough to be comfortable, say thirty-six inches. Now fill these frames with stones, smoothly polished, even sized, and let the content of the frame be even all about. Fill one frame with jade stones, fill one with malachite, fill one with jasper, fill one with emerald, one with topaz, one with amethyst, and so on . . . what a lovely order of beds you have now.

Go and lie in the jade bed of stones. Close your eyes. Allow yourself to know that it exists, and lie in it *now*. What do you feel? What do the stones give to you? Rise. Shower yourself in the shower nearby, and rest in the sun for a spell. Now go and lie down in the malachite bed for a while. Let your whole self lie there. Be there. Close your eyes and be totally there. Be with the healing stones. What do you feel? What do *these* stones give to you? Over a process of hours or days, visit all the beds of stones. Allow each one of them to give you its special qualities. Its special gifts it will gladly give to you if you will allow it . . . if you will open up and receive and allow yourself to become part of the stones and they become part of you.

You have now been healed through this process of sharing with the stones, and you have worked through other available processes also. Now is the time for you to make some decisions, some major ones. You take the crystal, the one held in hand, for you have come to that place where you want to know which path will bring the best benefit and health to all. You feel that your choice will affect many, for there is a closeness now between you and others, a bond has begun that feels like oneness. You strongly and sincerely desire to make the best choice for all.

You might draw a chart and hold the crystal in your hand. You plot on your map the possible choices. You hold the crystal, and working throught it you begin to divine the aspects of the choice. The physical qualities of the chart and the crystal obliterate themselves in the process of decision, and you become one with a knowing of the inner self, the greater self that dwells within.

Traveling on this energy, you move into your higher knowing, and the chart becomes a world you understand. You begin to see possibilities and options you had not seen before. Drawing on the small crystal energy and flowing through it, you divine and come to know as reality the decisions possible, and you see clearly as a path before you the best possible choice. The choice that would be best for all comes clear to you.

It is as a garden unfolding before you. You see the colors, the framework, and feel the feelings associated with it as you move into this new world you are creating. It excites you, because you can see the greater glory of it. You can see how this choice will be a healing for many.

You lay the crystal down, carefully placing it near its storage place in the sun, you let it rest to blend into itself the new elements it needs for its nourishment after its work. You close your eyes and say a prayer of thankfulness for this work done and this guidance received. Soon you will move about to carry out the objectives of the decision, but first the thank you. For as we send out, we receive, and we all wish to receive the best, the very highest force of which we are capable.

<><><><><>

"While divining choices, we move toward our goal with joy."

Lesson 10

THE COSMIC VEHICLE

For one moment, go back to the days of the quill pen. Here is the man sitting at his long-legged desk, writing with his quill. He dips the ink, writes on paper, dips, writes, dips, writes. Each time he dips, he has to make certain he collects the correct amount of ink, he wants no blotting, no scarcity. He wants his document to look good. He is a good writer, proficient. He handles the pen well. He is experienced. You step into the picture. You, with your modern clothes, step in. You are carrying a fine point, free-flow, rolling ballpoint pen. You hand it to him, showing him to write with it. He begins. Each time he automatically lifts his arm to dip the ballpoint into the ink well, you quickly place your palm over the well, not allowing him to dip. He questions, but understands and continues to write without dipping. He loves to write, and it is like a miracle to him, this writing without dipping. His document looks better than ever before. He holds it up when finished, and it looks so fine to him, so very fine. It is a miracle.

So, too, will the workings of the crystals look fine to you. They will look like miracles. There was the day of the quill point. There is the day of the ballpoint. Just as surely will come the day of crystals. And will they become as common as the ballpoint? They will. Not common in amount or usage, but in the minds of men and women they will become no more phenomenal than the ever-flowing pen. They will become a part of our conventional structure, as the rolling pen is now a part of it.

Built to last, these crystals will not dispense themselves, be used, and disappear as the pens, but they will be in common usage, and they will assist people daily at every task. It will be a new life. We will move from the days of fossil fuels into a life where we use cosmic energy more directly. Once a planet has been stepped up in vibration, it is closer to its source. It more nearly represents its source.

It can play havoc with its new energy if it wishes, or it can blend with *what is to be* and create with its Creator. If it chooses this latter task, it has many options, continuing into the forever-more. If it chooses its own will, it diminishes in size and disappears. Certainly, it takes many eons for this disappearance, but disappear it will, without cost. It will make no difference whether it existed or not . . . eventually.

If we are to live, and we are to live with our highest ability, we must realize our own holiness, our own right to life. Our choices are our *own* choices, where we can create our own worlds and inhabit them with that which we wish to coincide. In doing this, we create that which *we* create, and no other maker would create the same thing. It is our responsibility to make certain that which we create is good. If it is not good, we have gone afoul, and we must right our wrongs.

Here before us is a tremendous opportunity to right one of our wrongs. If we right it correctly this time, we will have a new world. If we right it incorrectly, we diminish in size almost to oblivion, for we have expanded into a new consciousness, and to erase it from our existence would leave little else to exist. The higher consciousness would move on, searching for a soul with which to coexist and we, the world, would be left as matter to be reprocessed. Let's not allow this parting of the two selves. Let's blend our Earth-retention self into our higher consciousness and coexist with our greater knowing, both body and soul. It can be done, and we are being given the challenge now. We *can* material-ize into the higher plane. It is quite possible. We must awaken our greater selves, get them moving into our daily consciousness, and allow them to take over the physical. It will be resplendent with joy, the physical, when we do. It will move with new abilities not known before. It will become a hallowed vehicle riding in a field of cosmic nourishment, as a bird flying in air, the sun on its wings, the wind at its back. In this cosmic vehicle, we will allow the transportation of the soul, and both will commingle with the knowledge that the life blood of superconsciousness is as a stem flowing into a rose: To sever the relationship is to die; to continue the bond, the pattern laid down, is to live and grow and seed once again the entire sphere until glory is met with glory, and the pattern is accomplished.

<><><><><>

"We are a cosmic vehicle that travels on waves of love."

PRACTICAL APPLICATION

W̶e have formed a healing center in our mind. Its main focal point is a blue crystal. Around this center point exists a live being, a vital force for healing. It consists of a physical plant, a home, cabins, natural paths for walking, "alone" spots where quietude and centering can happen. It has fresh water, good food . . . there are people about to lend assistance and give instructions when needed. It is a center of beauty, and much love is in solid operation here. It functions much as a clinic of the old days functioned, except with one tremendously important added feature: It is a whole being itself. It is complete unto itself, its health-giving force comes from within. It is a healthy being. If it senses or feels that part of it is becoming unhealthy, it stops its work and concentrates on bringing this part up to equal the health of the rest of its wholeness. In the meantime, those who have come to this center for healing echo this knowledge and in their own ways assist in this procedure of wholeness for all. It is a unit. There is unity here, there is closeness, openness. Each of us forfeits our individual knowing for the group, and it is found out that there is a group knowing that goes far beyond the individual knowing, and that it is good for all. Each of us pulls into ourself the understanding that as we move toward wholeness for ourself, we also move toward, and include into our understanding, oneness with all.

It is a picture that can be drawn in nature and it expands into the universe as a "unit of one." The same law applies to everyone and everything. Each fractal of energy pulls the same law into its gravitational field and must abide by its comprehension of balance if it is to continue to function as a center of knowing of long duration. The beingness simply fades, and its energy is drawn to other units that are closer to the law. The law is this, simply stated:

> When one and one
>   exist as One
> They survive.
>
> When one and one
>   exist as Two
> They diminish.

Energy feeding upon itself slows down its vibrational rate into nothingness. Energy commingling with another, so that the interaction between them draws the rays of the sun and increases them in activity, causes new life to be generated. This, then, is in abidance with the law and brings forth manifestations of cause. To cause is to create, and the first cause is also the last; and as surely as there is a first and a last, there is a forever.

In the blue crystal we see this forever. For have we not caused it to be born again into our midst? Have we not once again accepted the challenge? We have come a long way to find ourselves once again on the threshold of greatness. We have traveled many roads, come down many paths, and learned much. We have disciplined ourselves into rightness and we are ready to serve. We are ready to accept and understand that what we give to others we give to ourselves . . . that what we give is only that which is ourselves in others. We are ready to accept and understand that all beingness is one being, that all creation is one universe, that all that exists is us, and we are all.

Are we ready to work now . . . and to love? Are we ready to hear the call into greatness? Are we ready to follow it? One step . . . one step is all that is needed for commitment: the first step. The first step for many of us is crystals, working with crystals . . . this was our commitment, our promise. Are we ready?

This little book was written for you who made the crystal commitment. It is ready for you to use as a primer. It follows the blue crystal, does not speak of its secrets, but allows you to watch its unearthing and its flowering under the guidance of human beings. It is a beginning. It is only the beginning. From it can come greatness if we are willing to work.

Follow your lead. From where you are standing now there is one right direction, one right step to take. Take it. It will lead you to *your* crystal . . . for there is one for you. It may not be blue, it may be hues of pink, crystal clear, green, or shine with the gold of the sun; it may be small, it may be large. But whatever its description and wherever it is, it is yours and waits for you to unearth it in your time of finding. Your time of finding is not when you locate it. Your time of finding is when you find within yourself that duty performed which you promised to perform when you entered this time . . . this giving of self to others. It is this simple, to become *one* . . . to give and to receive, but to only know the giving.

We are here. We are ready. We serve. We are one. *Alam Selam*, go in peace.

◁▷◁▷◁▷

"Today, as we make practical application of all we know, we touch the earth with healing love."

THE CRYSTAL KEY

If one were told to climb a mountain and find a jewel so rare, if one were to happen upon a fine jewel that made the heart shine with memory . . . what then? Where does one move from here? To share increases the value of something dear to one's heart. To give of what we have that brings us joy, multiplies the joy. So we set about to share.

Having found the jewel, having erected it to its fullest potential for sharing, we ponder our next step of learning that we might be more knowledgeable in our sharing. For to teach is all well and good, but to teach with perfection brings a quality to both student and teacher that cannot be excelled. So let us aspire to learn our jewel well, that we might teach it, when the time comes, with depth of perception and excellence.

We trudge the hill as before. We stand in reverence before all that exists. We sense the birds strongly, the sun, the green of the softly moving leaves. We feel terra firma beneath our feet, and we feel a part of all that has been created. The birdsong blends itself into the music of the spheres and our jewel, our crystal, brings it home to us . . . brings our ability to tap this song and to share it. Not only is it a thing of beauty to the eye and to the touch, the ear now begins to pick up its song quite clearly. And relating it to the centers that sing within, we begin to imagine a kinship and an ability to communicate not thought of before.

So we stand back, eight or ten feet or more (depending on the size of the crystal), and begin to open the heart center to speak to the crystal. This first communication must be done gently and sensitively; for in the coming together we must match each other's vibrations, keenly aware that here is a powerful force tapped, and we must draw on it only according to our ability to control and handle it wisely.

So we open our heart center, and we communicate. What language does this crystal speak? Do we need to define our terms better to communicate with it? What kind of a conversation shall we have? Shall *we* lead, or shall we allow *it* to lead?

Always lead. Be the guardian and the forerunner. For in its depths are stored many memories. Many strengths may rise from its centers if you lead. However, if you were to allow *it* to lead, these strengths might fall wasted on the ground, for with your mind you control the power that is within the crystal. It has no mind of its own. It is dependent upon your mind to do correctly what must be done to bring it to its fullness. Do not think of it as mindless, however. Think of it rather as having a mind, and that mind is yours also. For once you have established communication with your crystal, you will not be the same as before. You will be a greater being, and the containments of your mind will include the crystal and all the memories that it stores. So, in a sense, *it* will become *your* teacher.

Now you might form a secret name for your crystal. Tell it to no one, but form in your heart a calling name with which you can communicate. This name is the right color, the right vibration, the right sound, and it calls to you the crystal consciousness and sets you in a pace equal to its pace, that you might partake of its stored knowledge.

Bordering on verbal conversation, this instruction from your jewel will come easily and automatically once you have learned the language. Giving the name will set the pace, so form it wisely. It will feel right once it *is* right, and you will know. Until this knowing comes, do not set it too firmly. Explore the vibrations and the sounds softly until you know. Then once you *know*, set the name firmly as you communicate in more depth. This name is your key to unlocking the power of the jewel and is to be shared with no one. *No one.* It is yours alone, and you are the master of this extension of your mind. You would no more lend this key than you would give away a portion of your mind into someone else's control. For you are building a relationship with a powerful force that is limitless in scope — powerful to the point of the possible extinction of the species, if it were used incorrectly. Yet used correctly, it can bring heaven-sent energy to nourish and instruct this planet into gladness never before known.

"The crystal key is in our heart of hearts; we will it forth."

THE CRYSTAL BUILDERS

Let us put aside the crystal experience for a moment and speak of our own growth. You have raised yourself to the point of crystal consciousness. You are able to communicate with your jewel. Quite freely, if haltingly, the flow of conversation comes now in broken words, but it comes consistently and with strength. You have established a point in your own consciousness where you are open to the crystal, and it in turn is open to you. In other words, you have built in your mind an area, an *in*-point, reserved for communication with your crystal, and this is its only function. This in-point is a newly functioning part of you. This area of contact was reserved in your brain when you were born. You built it into yourself for this purpose. It is largely for this purpose that you came in this time. There are others like you. You are a network of your own. You are the crystal builders.

So once you have established this contact with your jewel, once you have touched soul to soul, what then? Spend much time in each other's presence in silence . . . and in gentle conversation. Get used to each other. And here comes the growth on your part: You will begin to feel inside yourself a new awareness of all things. You will begin to feel like a new person, an extended person from what you were before. You will sense things not physically sensed, and they will come with an awareness that is knowing, yet wondering. You will have in your mind, your new mind, a consciousness of things about you that you did not have before. You will rise in the morning and feel completely different.

You will have a power about you not felt before. You will be drawing on the crystal energy.

As you realize this new strength, be careful. Be cautious; test it as you go, step by step. Keep yourself pure. Lift your thoughts and your actions high. Hold them aloft for the blessing of the Son every morning, and ask for guidance in this pursuit. You are on a mighty mission, one that holds power and responsibility. You must do this task well, for a world waits for your bidding, and those of you in the crystal network hold an awesome amount of power. It is thus essential that you build yourselves well. Each individual soul must listen to his or her own conscience and build his or her heart in the right place for this mission. For we are building a new heaven and a New Earth, and the New Earth is as the old Earth, and the new heaven is *out* of the old Earth. So rest in peace, those who choose to remain with the old Earth made new, and build in joy, those who temper the new heaven.

As you grow, you mature in wisdom, and it is wisdom that you need to be the wise benefactor of a new nation. There will be many such, and you must grow equal in nature, in habits, and in love if you are to keep your network stable, if you are to keep your energy flourishing one to another as you grow into the Christ consciousness that is the establishment of the new nation. For did we not come in love this time to found a new creed and a new way of behavior for humanity? We did, and in this new way we each must individually grow if we are to lead others by our example and with our assistance. For we came to grow mightily, and we must pursue this path now if we are to be on schedule for the new awakening and the new enlightenment of our planet Earth.

So as you sit with your jewel in quiet communication and contemplation, know that you are growing within and consciously guide this inner newness. Direct it to become the higher you, with habits that befit the new consciousness. Rise daily with joy. Keep the body healthy. Practice love. Watch out for those habits that are stubborn and those that would have you forsake your way of purity. Keep the thoughts high and the love flowing and when a mistake is made, and the soul creeps in upon itself to hide, bring it out with joy again. Admonish it and step forward again to practice and to achieve. For it is for this purpose we came in. We have built ourselves for this mission. It is our task. We had best be about it.

⬦⬦⬦⬦⬦

"We are crystals builders come forth to work on planet Earth."

THE LONGING HEART

There is within you a goal set at birth. A vibration is set up within you by your choice and designing, and it resonates in a calling to your higher self . . . constantly. Every human has this from birth, *every* human. It is a microcosm of the greater self and sets the pattern of the life. When one moves out of this pattern, one feels uncomfortable. When one flows with this pattern, there is joy in one's life. Albeit there are many variations of the same pattern, there is one true pattern for each soul, and the closer one adheres to this master plan, the more joy comes forth.

Each soul designs its own pattern before entering for the experience, designs it with growth in mind for its own being, designs it for service to others, which is the key to growth. With the soul when it designs its pattern are many friends and helpers. Coworkers abound in this universe, and we design our plans to fit in with one another's, so we might assist each other in our disciplines of growth and service. We are united in many ways, and this is by far the most potent union. It makes us one. For when you are committed to each other's growth, when you have designed yourself to turn and turn once again with other souls to your completion, you are indeed a unit. (A unit soul is sometimes spoken of as souls that travel in groups, but both terms refer to the same concept.)

So if you design your own plan, and you design it in conjunction with others, what does this set up inside you as you enter the plane and proceed with your life? From birth you have within you the longing heart. Resonating within is that microcosm, that tiny symbol, that fractal of your greater self, and it calls to you constantly to match its pace. It is the longing heart. Forever it rings true to the greatest potential. Constantly it sets the pace, and all that resonates with it is comfortable to the soul, and all that is discordant with it makes the soul uncomfortable. It is a modern, scientific miracle. It is ingenious . . . and it works. It has not always been thus. It is a rather recent invention of the last few thousand years, and is yet to be perfected.

Within the soul abides this trigger, and it is working. It brings to us our own stability and our own awareness of our needs. It helps us measure and balance our own whereabouts and assists us in designing our path for the next few measures. We design as we go. The details in the overall pattern are laid down, but we must forge the plan daily that leads us to our completion.

It might interest you to know that much of this daily planning is done at night when you are asleep. For your dreams are naught but your greater awakening, and while you sleep, you plan your day, and you do this in conjunction with others. Your soul unit gathers nightly, and together it plans the activities of the adjoining few days, months, and years, varying the patterns as needed to match the experiences encountered.

When we enter, we have a plan, and we make variations of this plan as we refine it. It is always a perfect plan for the cause when we design it, but alterations must always be made; for we work in an area that does not always respond perfectly to our calling. Such is the Earth plane.

Now to dwell on Earth causes one to wonder, "Where *is* the plan? Does *any* of this make sense?" Well, it *all* makes sense, *all* of it. For every action is a variation of the master plan, and that master plan resides within each of us fully blown, as in a tiny capsule in our center of centers, and it is known fully to our heart. For within each of us is the knowledge that we have a purpose, a mission; and as we direct ourseles toward this mission, we feel well and fulfilled. As we direct ourselves away from this purpose, we feel depleted and causeless.

So in your heart know that you have a cause. It is there by your choice, your designing. It is there for a purpose that touches all humankind. It is no little cause, this choice you made. Prepare yourself, search out your cause. Long to know its purpose, its quest. You will find it. It will come to you as you search for it. It is yours and yours alone, and fits in conjunction with those of your coworkers. You will not be working alone. There are many of us committed to this task. We have built our jobs in harmony with one another, and they will mesh together like a miracle from heaven, for that indeed is what they are.

◇━◇━◇━◇━◇

"We follow our longing hearts to oneness."

Lesson 15

THE EMPOWERED FRACTAL

In fractals we see the universe reflected as we might see a rainbow reflected in a drop of water. A fractal is that which has no duplicate smaller than it is, yet it represents and is represented by thousands upon thousands of duplicates in the universe, great and small. A fractal is a pattern, yet it is a pattern that exists in fullness to be exploded many times into oneness, for it represents that which is all and contains within itself the exact and complete pattern of the whole.

Now, as we consider fractals, as we study them, we come to understand that once we have mastered the comprehension of the point of power of the fractal, we have mastered all. For within the fractal is the secret of the entire universe and once you have understood the fractal dynamics, you have tapped the universal source.

Now where are these fractals? In the tip of your thumb, in the bone of your leg, in the hair on your head, in the food you ate for supper . . . all are fractals and groups of fractals. A fractal is a map of the universe; it is the universal pattern in completeness. If you shrunk the universe until there was only one fractal left, within that fractal would be the universe. Do you see the power contained here? From one fractal you can create a universe . . . and there are thousands of fractals in the tip of your thumb.

So what power do you hold? None, if you do not *understand* fractals; all power, if you comprehend the workings of a fractal and can cooperate with it to explore, create, and control.

Visualize a light beam in front of you, a few feet away. What color is this light beam? Give it a color. Now stabilize it in space, and as you do, will it to bend. Bend this light beam until you have part of it perpendicular to the original flow. Hold it there for a moment. What do you learn by studying it? You have before you a bent light beam. You chose the color, you chose the placement, you chose the bending. Now, stabilizing this beam and holding it firmly in front of you, unbend it. Bring it back to its original shape. Hold it there. Slowly change its color. Bring it up the scale or down the scale in vibration until you have it clearly a different color. Hold it there.

What have you been doing? You have been transforming crystals. And in this transforming of crystals, you have been manipulating fractals. Why fractals of light? They are easier to bend than the physical. They are more malleable and respond more fully to mind control than does the denser physical. Look back at your beam. Is it still there? Has it faded? Give it renewed energy. Sight it again in your vision. Hold it there. Feed it energy. Nourish it with the fractals of your mind until it becomes more dense. Can you make it real? Could others see it as you do? Make it so real that your neighbor walking in the door could see it and comment, "What is this you have in the middle of the room? Could I have one?"

Now rest your mind. Let the beam of light evaporate, and rest your mind. Do not become too fond of it, for it is a light source that is always at your fingertips and is constantly changing. You change it with your actions and your mind and you can use it at will to create what you choose to create. It is, in a sense, your fractal of light, that which surrounds you as your creative force. It is as no other, yet it is set in the pattern of all. It responds only to those laws that govern all, and outside of these laws it cannot exist. It is a fractal pattern within a larger fractal pattern, and it has fractals within it. It is duplicated beyond itself and within itself and you can control it as a beam of light in the mind and in space in front of you. You can control it. It is yours to practice with, it is yours to build with. It is yours and you govern it within the laws that are laid down for all fractals.

No cell of your body can exist without these laws, and you can govern each cell as you control the beam of light, if you wish to. The mind is the builder, and it builds as it projects what it desires. If it desires failure, it projects failure, and it has failure. If it desires success, it thinks success, and it has success. Each accomplishment is maintained and held in the mind before it becomes a fact. Each fact must be nourished by mind to continue to exist. If it is not nourished, it fades away, it evaporates.

Now do you see the power in the fractal? Do you see the power you might have, if you learn the secret of the fractal, the pattern from which all existence springs? Do you choose to work with your fractal of light until you explore it into something powerful and good . . . your own creation? Multiplied, that fractal can do either harm or good. It is your choice. Which do you choose?

◇◁◇◁◇◁◇

"We empower fractals of light with our minds; together we speak love."

CHRIST CONSCIOUSNESS

The fractal that we see in our mind's eye is a perfect pattern. If you want to see it triangular in nature, with the sun shining through it as a prism of glass, this image would be true to the form and nature of the fractal. Yet hold it closer, and gaze into its center. Let the light play on the colors within it, and see the reflections and the frames of reference that it contains. If you wish, take a manmade silver crystal, and hold it aloft on a chain. See the scene in its interior; see the images that are formed there by the combination of the sun and the crystallized energy that swings from the chain. What do you see? The rainbow frequently edges, covers, devours, flirts with, pierces, bounces off of the prisms within the prism.

Now what of this rainbow? What does it contain? It contains the whole and it is brought down into your viewing, into your spectrum of light, by the little silver crystal made by the hand of a person. What magic is this, that little particles placed in a certain arrangement should reflect the glory of all? A fractal is the smallest pattern known of the all. A rainbow is evidence of that pattern in the physical. For the rainbow is one triangle of light beside another triangle of light beside another, beside another and another and another; and each one is bending to the will of the others so they all might in harmony present their spectrum of perfection to the sun which produces them in the physical.

Now the Son comes to produce in the physical the full spectrum, the divine all, the wholeness, the oneness of humankind.

With each of us yielding our will for the benefit of all, we will produce in our hearts, in our minds, in our soul beings that which is the pattern, that which is the Christ consciousness. For he was and is the pattern. He is the fractal for humankind. In him did we see on Earth the physical pattern which we are all to follow if we are to produce our own rainbows of light, our own fractals of completion, our own basic unit of goodness that is perfect in design, perfect in behavior, and perfect in the expression of love. For in our wills we find the reason to yield our personal need to that which fits the needs of all, and in so doing we become basic and complete units of the divine Godhead which produces all, contains all, and lives in all and with all. We are fractals of God, as was Christ when he walked in the body of Jesus on this planet Earth to set the pattern. Of our own need and in our hearts we respond to this calling to become fractals in the living unit of God, and we see that not only do we have the desire, but we also have the ability, and we must do it now while the melting pot of the creation bends its rainbow light our way for our nourishment in this cycle.

So as you hold the silver crystal aloft and see in it the rainbow effect, know that in your heart, in your center, shines a greater rainbow, and it was built there by you for the coming of the Christ consciousness into your soul, your being of beings, and that now is the time to activate it and let it shine in the Son.

Your crystal on the hill will be the instrument with which you share your rainbow with all other human rainbows, and you will see the day when the Earth is ringed with rainbows and love shines in the hearts of all humanity.

<>=<>=<>=<>=<>

"Christ consciousness is all we know and all we are meant to be."

Lesson 17

THE MINERAL BEDS

In the human being resounds a certain knowledge of the mineral content of the planet Earth. This mineral content is not limited only to the planet Earth; but a certain quality, a uniqueness, a specific arrangement, is due only to the planet building herself as the planet Earth. This vibrational force is echoed in other spheres, but is not found in this complete arrangement elsewhere. Therefore, there is a uniqueness and a stability that is not found elsewhere, and it also resounds in the cells of the human beings who inhabit the planet Earth.

Being part mineral, and therefore part of Earth, human beings are designed to sustain themselves on Earth as living beings. In the balance of things, it is essential that you keep your content and your quality in a certain arrangement of particles in order to produce optimum health—that is, an optimum functioning of all parts in relationship to other parts, that all might produce the desired effect of harmony in functioning and in production, if production is desired.

If the physical body is healthy, if it functions in optimum health, all parts working together for the good of all, then the soul resides with comfort and can do its work well. If the physical is in a condition where there is a drawing one part on another because of an imbalance of need and satisfaction, then the soul has great difficulty sustaining itself and going forth with its work to produce. So it is paramount at this time to find ways to keep the physical body healthy to an optimal degree. It is more important now than it has *ever* been, because we are attempting to bring the divine nature, which vibrates at a higher rate, more into the physical, and we plan to do it through the human being. We cannot do so if you do not find ways to keep your body physically healthy . . . ways that work in an enduring nature . . . ways that are acceptable, practical, and possible in these times of great change. We have been researching, investigating additional effects that would assist you in this climb of your soul self joining your conscious self in the physical in full force and knowledge.

To keep healthy, one must see that all parts of the physical receive what they must to sustain themselves for the job they must do. The mineral kingdom—the stones, the rocks, the ledges, the soil, the living waters that run with minerals in them—all these sources of sustenance are more important to humans than they used to be. You are lifting your consciousness to a point where you can sustain yourself less with the animal matter and more with that which enters directly into the bloodstream as life substance itself. When you eat, energy has to be converted. When you eat meat, the energy is converted through a process of slow digestion rather than rapid assimilation, and that slows down the vibratory rate that we are attempting to speed up.

Here we can refer to the beds of polished stones. If we bathe and then rest on a bed of polished amethyst warmed by the sun, what consequence is this? How does this nourish us? How can this—indeed, *can* this—make the body physically more healthy, more balanced? Yes. You must see that many, *many* people have raised themselves to the point where they can no longer comfortably abide the eating of flesh. Some are in the transition state where they can still tolerate partaking of some meat, but are finding that they are in a process of withdrawing, that it is taking some time; but they are aware that animal matter no longer has the desired effect on them it used to, and they are less and less frequently consuming it.

So, can we raise our vibrations and absorb a type of mineral content by lying in a bed of amethyst? "Ridiculous!" you say. Not so. The higher vibrational field you are in, the more you absorb that which is around you. And with conscious intent, a high-minded person might "partake" of a fine mineral meal by going from a bed of amethyst to jade, to coral, to ruby, and so on until he or she felt the acceptable balance achieved.

Now we will confess that in addition to absorbing this mineral content, you also achieve many other goals—and perhaps the absorption of the needed minerals is not even the greatest or most intense experience you will have in this process of moving from one bed of polished stones to another. Perhaps other fields of knowing are being affected . . . and they are. But first we must understand that to do it for the body's self alone would be sufficient reason: for we are changing that body from one of gross matter to one of light, and in this process, we are keeping the physical intact. Do you understand?

So contemplate, as you become more knowledgeable about your jewel on the hill: Contemplate the effects of abiding near stones, contemplate the reason for living in nearness to crystals, and contemplate your role in building crystal beds or beds of polished stone that might be used for healing. As you contemplate, it will come about, for it is much needed for the raising of your understanding of your physicality and how it ties in with the soul being that you are, and how you can program yourself into physical wellness—the wellness that you must achieve if you are to harbor or even live with your day consciousness awake and alive to your greater self, your soul being that knows no barrier between yourself and the divine.

⬦⬦⬦⬦⬦

"We are of the soil of the Earth, and we are divine."

Lesson 18

THE WELLSPRING

Now, why have we not gotten to more of the specifics? *You are the specifics. Remember, please, this is a primer. It is for your benefit that we write this. You have a calling, you have a need to fulfill.* Somewhere within you resounds a knowing that you have a specific job to do. Now if it revolves around the material contained in this book, you will benefit greatly, not by reading it, but by building on the knowledge that comes to you from your inner knowing as you read it. When you read this book, know that within you is a reservoir of knowledge much vaster than that which could be contained in a book. You have within you a growing knowledge that out of the depth of your knowing you can use this well of information and expand on it as if it had already happened. Compressed within you, already spun, is a universal construction larger than the information written here. And you are to feed, to fuel, that construction, give it life and growth, by fueling yourself with these words.

Now let's return to the blue crystal and see how she is doing in her progress. To communicate with humanity is her goal, and to tie into your systems so that she might be of help with your creation. She is nondemanding and noncontrolling. She wishes to serve . . . but a more powerful servant has not been known. Even in the dimensions of the atomic power field, there is no more power-filled servant. Recognize this, and you are off to a good start. Acknowledge this power, and act wisely in this knowing, and all will go well.

It is your mind that is the instrument of perfection. It is your mind that must be disciplined and precise. It is your mind that is to empower and control this crystalline power. A crystal lying dormant by itself is not a powerful instrument. Only in conjunction with your mind is it powerful. The two combined — your creative mind and the composed, concentrated energy pattern of the crystal — make an unequaled planning board and energy source. There is greater fine tuning available in this combination than has heretofore been thought possible. There is greater resonance possible between creator (you) and instrument of application (the crystal) than has been acknowledged or implemented before.

So here she is, our blue crystal. Risen above the soil that once enclosed her, she is now polished, harnessed in her frame of gold and copper, and she is ready to produce. She gleams in the sun as it falls in dappled patterns through the leaves, and deep within her blueness are unanswered questions and hints of awesome strength and ability, still hidden. She is helpless without your love. Four feet in length and nineteen inches in breadth, she is heavy for her size, concentrated, and you sense that within her is a well that reaches into eternity. And well you might consider this, for combined with your energy, this is true of her. In your knowing of her you have respect — not to the point of worship like the ancients, nor love for her either — but respect and awe, for you have not yet earned her friendship . . . neither has she earned yours.

The love you must acquire is not for her alone, but for the eternity she represents and for the masses that she and you have promised to serve. Dedicated to turn again your knowledge into one another's keeping, you have sworn to keep it clean this time, to tell it straight and to broadcast with love the benefits of your knowing, using your combined abilities to further the progress of humankind on its way to seeking its Godhead, its eternal now.

She is your wellspring of knowledge for your calling, this crystal, and you can read her like a computer. She will issue printouts for you like you have not known before, because they will be part of your blood and your desire. The sensitive recording paper will be your brain tissue, the ink will be your memory. Your creative, exploring mind empowered by desire and guided by love will build on the knowledge gained from this living printout, and you will construct that which must be for the benefit of all.

So we have sat in deep meditation with this crystal. We have touched her surface, admired her flaws and perfections alike, and wondered as to her powers . . . and her promise. We are becoming aware of other crystals. We've heard rumors of them, yet unseen in the flesh, we see them in dreams at night. Some gold, some green, some ruby red, some clear and multiribboned with rainbows, we sense they are forming a network, *have* formed a network. We hear the glimmerings of it in our sleep, and we respond to it in our waking by learning love in our daily lives, learning kindness, and sitting with our crystal in meditation and communication.

The garden is well formed now. In the future it may be much grander, but for now we have raked and cleaned and planted to our own liking, and we are getting a sense of the energy in the area and how it can be used. We are acquiring a sensitivity to the flows and pulls of motion in the surrounding area, and we are discovering the land and what power it holds in specific places. We are beginning to see a pattern, still vaguely, but it is beginning to dawn on us that we have much to learn, and part of this learning is in the form of a pattern that repeats itself over and over again. Once we learn the pattern, once we pattern ourselves after it, in love, learning will become easier, and remembering will become a thing of the past, because we will know what *is* and what must be done *now*.

Do you begin to see the use of the crystallized energy? Do you begin to feel the calling within you? Do you begin to sense where *your* crystal might be and what specific use it might have? Is it a healing crystal used for the physical body or for the emotions? Is it a crystal honed for mental astuteness and for the training of the mind? Is it for generating heat or power of the kind to run machines both in the physical and in the etheric? Is it for pulling loads? Is it for communications only? What *is* your specialty? What *is* your interest? Where does *your* promise lie? What was *your* specific commitment?

Within you is a knowing. Within you is an answer to all of the questions you have ever asked. Within you is eternity. You *are* eternity. As you revolve and evolve and change and create, you find each of your callings . . . and now is the time of "crystals come forth," and you turn once again to the basic level of creating. We are creating once again a mass, a new planet in a new dimension and with this creating, the crystals bridge the gap. It has been called the rainbow bridge, and it *is*—for it holds, full spectrum, the formation of a place to live for those who have come to their crystal consciousness, to that place where all work together for the good of all. We build knowledgeably together that which must be to suit all.

We are entering an age of enlightenment, and that which is will fade away, as that which is meant to be presents itself. To walk this bridge, this bridge between *matter* and *nonmatter combined with matter*, we must use the crystal, we must activate it fully and use it for all its worth in all its glory and with love. For the crystalline power is one of the keys to our future, the future that we planned to create and which now we are creating.

◁▷◁▷◁▷

"We are wellsprings of eternity; we know the answers."

Lesson 19

THE NEW PLANET

The blue crystal is our model. Our application will come later, when we each find our own individual crystal. You are blessed to have before you a plan, a pattern, of that which is to come. These times are rare. These times when we are faced with a knowledge that we cannot describe, but which we know with full certainty is coming into our experience, our consciousness . . . these times are rare. We move forward. We endeavor to grasp with some measure of understanding the coming times and our indebtedness to them. We long for more understanding, that we might be more productive *now*. We are frustrated. Things seem to be in some way out of sync. We are confused about the present and the past. The future seems to be here and yet not here. Our centeredness suffers.

Abide this confusion. It is a point of growth. It is the you that is straining to become the you that is to be. It is your memory catching up with your present and your future calling to your present to give it energy and incentive. It is the power of your all calling to you more clearly than ever before, and it is the *you that is to be* moving into your present, the eternal now.

So abide this confusion. It is short-lived, and soon you will be too busy to let it bother you. Soon you will be handling devices, controlling energies, and building that which in your wildest dreams you did not envision building. For no one has seen and no ear heard that which really is to be. We can perceive that which is, and our imaginations can bounce off of that which we know and attempt to construct in our reaching, desiring minds that which is to be. But the glory of what is to come, the absolute total of our potential, that which we do as we build, we have yet to understand.

Does a little child looking under the Christmas tree correctly envision the contents of the brightly wrapped gifts? No, each package holds something hidden, something special, something not known. And as the child dreams of the glory to come, the day of opening, so can we dream of what might be if we build correctly. But ear has not heard nor eye seen the glory that is to come.

We build a planet that is so glorious. We build a place for ourselves that is so untold as to be unimaginable. There will be spaces that are not spaces in our new home. There will be places that are nonplaces. Yet they will be real and usable, and we will be comfortable with them, and they will provide us with the substance we need for our growth and our creation to be. We will walk from one dimension into another as we now walk from the bus stop to the corner, and we will feel no difference . . . only that we now have a new function, a new way of behaving, a new ability to relate, to perceive, and to create. There will be clouds that are pools, and pools that are stones, and stones that are beings, and beings that are both animal and angel. There will be grasses that talk and birds that swim and suns that shine both day and night. There will be sisters and brothers, layer upon layer of them, thousands of souls that visit us daily, and we will feel no exhaustion, for we will be expanded and our consciousness will comprehend and interact in ways that we are now unable to understand. There will be blues where there are greys, and greens where there are golds, and purples will blend with pinks as we have not seen before. Yet we will understand the definition of each color and each individual duty and use. We will understand much better than we do now, for we will see more with our all and we will have caring for the all more clearly in our hearts than we do now.

And, my dears, the crystal is our tool of comprehension and use. We build anew using the crystal. So get on with your studies. Do your disciplines, which you have committed yourself to. Learn love, proceed with kindness, and do this day what must be done. Develop your life into what it must be for you to serve to your very highest degree. Move forward with faith and with hope and know that you create anew that which was created as of old, yet you sing a new song, and you build a new city. *Alam Selam*, go in peace. We build with you.

⬦⬦⬦⬦⬦

"We are a rainbow bridge; our hands mold the new planet as our toes still touch the old."

Lesson 20

THE PROMISE

The love pours forth from a center so large that it encompasses all. The movement is from time, and the substance is from space. Yet there is no such thing as time and space. These are just human definitions to aid in the comprehension of the movement of the all. So what do we see when we look at the all through the fractal of the crystal?

We see empowered here a resonance that beats with the rhythm of the universe. We see at our doorstep an object, a mere physical object, which is empowered with the substance of the universe. For is it not beating with the same rhythm? Is its substance not composed of the same matter, and is its pattern not exactly that of its Creator, the universal one?

So if you take time and expand it to nontime, and if you take space and expand it to nonspace . . . and if you take patience, the acceptance of the fact that you see only a short distance before you . . . if you take these three — time, space, and patience — you will have the beginning of the answer that empowers your crystal in your knowing.

For was it not in the beginning that you asked to be a creator? Did you not cry out, "My God, my God, why have you forsaken me," and asked to be let back in so that you might create beside your God? Did you not in faith and in substance promise to do it right this time? To evaluate correctly and to weigh and to keep your feet on the right path that you might rectify the bending of the points that you caused in your carelessness? Did you not set aside some "time," declare some "space" to withdraw and correct? And now have you not come forth with your banners of faith, your memory, and your longing, and are you not ready to build anew that which you destroyed?

You are! You are ready. You have come forth and you have brought with you that which is buried deep in your soul being. In *your* knowledge is that which is to come forth, and it cannot come forth, it cannot issue itself into creation without you. Do you believe this? Do you *really* believe this? You had better. For on *your* shoulders does the debt lie. In your hands is the mold cast. By your shape, your promise, your forthrightness is it formed, this new creation.

Are you a builder? Do you recognize your value and your worth? Are you ready to take up the sword, and with the energy of the universe point that sword in one direction and have it stay? Do you want this job, this responsibility?

It is yours without your asking. For you have built yourself into it. You would not be, if it were not for the building of this plan. It was your promise, your point of being, and your life. With this plan you breathed life into yourself, and by carrying out this plan will you create your whole self.

You are on the right track. You have found the right road. You are reading the signposts correctly. You are not fooling yourself this time.

You no longer have the ability to fool yourself, for you have brought the mental and the physical to a place of meeting where they can no longer separate themselves from one another and survive. They would fracture into basic elements were they to try to stand on their own without the assistance of your *body-mind-spirit* to support them.

Now what does all this mean? What are all these superlatives and exclamations?

It is simply this: Defined as the person who came out of the cold, you have surrounded yourself with such fine energy, such radiance, that you can no longer function as a human, but must take upon you the robe of divine being, clothe yourself in the Spirit that becomes you, and move into your new state of beingness.

You have formed a new world and into the world you must move, for it calls you as your own, and your vibrations no longer match the old; it would shatter before you stepped on it. It is no longer for you. The new is before you. There is no turning back. The old has moved to its station of forgiveness, and it is for others, not you. It will serve well those who follow it. You are a new being, and Light shines through you as water did before, and your age has come.

Be aware that at your feet is the working tool, the crystal. Your new life brings to you the power to control universal energies in a way that you have not mastered before. Rise to the cause. Accept your burden. Remember your promise, and step forth with understanding and with love. You have cause to be. You are a part of the Creator. You are worthy. You are precious beyond compare. You are life.

For in the greater pattern, there is a pattern, and their colors blend perfectly. The movement to and fro from large to small and from small to large again is seen as a perfection of change. For behold, the wind blew forth onto the face of the waters, and all things that had transgressed were brought home again, and all beings became one being, and all light became one light. For as was promised, the lamb shall lie down with the lion, and a little child shall lead them.

⋄⋄⋄⋄⋄

"The promise, which we remember, leads us to that which we would build."

Lesson 21

THE FOREVER NOW

In the heart there has been set up a longing that brings it to its goal, its destination. As a homing signal calling to its own, it sends out evenly spaced, constant charges of orange energy like beads flying through the sky to call its own to itself. It is a kind of sonar, yet it is more powerful than the sonar that defines space. This heart energy has the ability to construct a web in which to entangle and sort out that which it needs to build its desire.

We have been taught the heart is the organ that pumps blood through the circulatory system. It is this truly. In its finer body, it extends this function into a greater range, into vaster reaches of the universe—yes, the universe—and it pulls to itself those energies it needs to construct its greater self. It can be seen as a larger circulatory system, if you wish, for it brings to itself the needed substance to nourish its greater body. Revolving and revolving, taking its turn at the platform where work must be sent out to produce, it harnesses that which must be harnessed in order to construct the being that is to be, the holy one that will become the wholly one.

We work towards perfection. And what is perfection? Perfection is the part working as an integral element of the whole. It is the fractal expressing itself as the greater part. It is the harmony of the small interacting with the large in such a way as to enhance the function of the all and therefore glorify the beingness of creation, the song of the universe.

"What then?" you say. "What if we reach this perfection? What do we do then? What's to hold our interest?"

Imagine a stream running in the woods. It is a most beautiful stream. Torrents of fast-running water splash over rocks. Trees bow and limbs shake to the breeze that it carries. Flowers grow by its side. Animals come to its wider pools to drink. An occasional waterfall falls a few inches to splash water below in musical tones. But you see an opportunity, an opportunity for change. You see that here, here in this spot you've wandered to, a deeper waterfall could be built. By easily moving a few large stones and replacing some of the soft mud, you could have, instead of a five-inch waterfall, a four-foot waterfall. The idea intrigues you. The vision of a more impressive sight enhances your feeling of excitement and beauty. So you construct, you change, you rearrange, and you come up with something that pleases you. Not to say that the stream wasn't perfection before you started to work on it, but to say that you have within you the ability to create . . . and that your creation is *your* creation with your mark, your signature on it, your energy power within it, and yours to behold as beautiful. Yours to share.

Do you see now why the universe is so fluid? Do you see why change is a constant? Do you see the beauty of all that is and all that is to be? Do you see the meaning of "that which is to come"?

A little flower grows from the soil. Once a seed, it blossoms into its fullness as the sun draws it upward and the atmosphere nourishes it; the surrounding area yields to its needs. As this little flower, which turns itself into a seed again, can we grow. Destined to be ever changing, destined to be the flow within the eternal flow, we seek perfection. We seek our place in the Son, because we are a fractal of the whole, and we long to feel around us the warmth of *that which is*. We want to be one with it, to sing the same song, to harmonize in our tone with the masterpiece of creation.

In your crystal you will see this complete cooperation. Otherwise, it would not have become a crystal. It is the gem of gems of the mineral kingdom. Learn from it. Take within your instruction the basic knowledge that you must hold to learn to operate your crystal, to cooperate with your power source, your transformer, called a crystal.

Know this . . . that as you develop in your sense of "what is," as you expand your understanding of "that which is to come," you get more fully in touch with "that which is meant to be," and you see visions correctly of what must be done to achieve these ends. So work with your crystal, sit with it, meditate with it, follow your inner knowing as to what to do to instruct yourself in its greater knowing. There will be classes to take, books to read, skills to learn. There will be people to meet, bridges to cross, and substances to apply. There will be all manner of gatherings to come forth and networks to weave. There is work to do. Begin now.

◇━◇━◇━◇━◇

"We are the now moment; the forever now is what we are."

Lesson 22

THE WORKING CYCLE

When we consider that all the world is a unit, it makes us wonder what is wrong with our vision, because there is much that we see that does not look unified to us. "Unity is a scarce thing," we say, "It is hard to come by. There is much disharmony."

Now, wait a minute. Pause and draw back from the scene. Remove yourself from it for a moment. Become an observer, undistracted by the limiting factors of emotions, and consider: What is your vision? Do you create what you see? How much power do you have?

We have drawn a circle around ourselves. We see so far and no farther. You in your human realm have the vision to see that which is three-dimensional. You designed yourself this way for a purpose. You have a job to do within that limited functioning, and you can do it correctly only with the circle of human perspective drawn around you to cut off the view, the knowledge, of what is to be in reality. So you operate in a world unknown to you. You see portions and allotments. You seldom see the whole. Were you to see the whole, if only in glimpses, you would be moving above your human vision, so to speak, and you would be seeing with your third eye, which we must admit is not entirely human.

We play with words here to get across a point: To be human is to have chosen to limit one's ability and vision for a specific task, a dedicated service. This choice is to be honored. All manner of praise needs be given those souls who take it upon themselves to serve in this way. To work with limited vision is not a choice easily made. Much thought and planning, much consultation with others is needed and progressed through before the final choice is made. Then must the soul divide itself into parts and extract its functions one from another and send part of itself, to the Earth planet to function as a whole, when in reality it is only a fractal.

Do you begin to see now why you see disharmony where really there is the grandest of harmonies? Do you see that as human, you see only the part and not the whole? . . . Therefore what you perceive appears to be fractious, but in reality, if you were to see the whole design, it would be glorious to behold, this universe of harmonies.

So what good does it do to contemplate what isn't? *I can't see it, therefore it isn't. What I see I can work with. What I cannot see, I cannot work with. It is that simple.*

Yes, it is that simple, and more simple still. For what is to you in your vision, your human vision, is what you are meant to work with. It is what you have chosen as your work, and your tools are all about you. You sometimes call them frustrations . . . or challenges, if you are in a better mood. These are your tools, the objects of what you promised to do when you chose this mission, this life, this time on this planet Earth.

So when you consider that all the world is a unit and that just beyond your sight is the explanation of all that is which ties all together . . . know that you have work to do, that what is before you must be done before you will see further.

When you hear the sharp tin can rolling noisily in the dirty alley, when the nights are too hot and the days bring unexpected changes that you feel you did not request, know that you requested them. Know that within you is a desire so strong to set things straight, to line up the fractals on this planet so they will mesh with the finer fractals, that the tool you need to work with to do your job calls to you constantly.

You are a millwright in the bowels of the mill, fine-tuning the huge machinery so that above the looms might weave the finer cloth, the linens and the woolens into the usable, understand-able fabric of existence for all to use.

So come with your knowing into your task, and with your eyes open call to your third eye, your higher mind, to understand that which is above, on the higher floors of this universal mill. Work knowing that you have limited your sight for a purpose, a cause. Work knowing that you chose this service in the bowels of the mill out of love for your fellow kind. Work knowing that you are doing a good job as long as you are able to keep your spirits high and carry love in your knowing and in your doing.

In wisdom you must set forth. We impart this section about the whole and the part and your choice of limited vision that you might more clearly see beyond that which you have chosen. For the time has come for the expansion of the awareness, and that which was not seen must be seen for us to carry out our mission in harmony, side by side with hand assisting hand, as we build the new planet. Have faith, take courage. We are pioneers, and we are going forth with strength. A bond is being formed. In all our service we have never seen anything so beautiful. Keep working. Please.

⬦⬦⬦⬦⬦

"We create joyfully in this day's vision."

Lesson 23

DEDICATION

We have come and shared much with you in the last few lessons. Are you becoming more comfortable with us? We would share with you now a picture we see from our point of vision:

See a human body, please, a rather frail human body, female in nature. Envision it sitting at a desk and writing. The surroundings are quite acceptable, quite beautiful. In the right there is a balcony overlooking a huge window, and the window looks out onto miles of tree-studded terrain and beyond that the blue mountains and the sky. The sun shines, the birds sing, the flowers grow, the streams flow. All is well with nature, it seems. It is clearly an Earth scene we have brought to our vision, and we want to help you see it through our eyes—we who are committed to working with you humans, just above your sphere, in the next few finer dimensions.

This female body has a tenuous hold on Earth life; that is why we call it frail, although most humans would see it as rather strong and hail. But we, because of our choice of position, see more clearly than you, and we see the connections more clearly. We are not more developed than you, many of us. You are more "developed" than you think. It is only that your knowledge of yourself is temporarily more limited. You chose the short sight, for you have a job to do, a mission to carry out.

So we will help you see in these few pages what you look like through our eyes, from our vantage point . . . and if you were here with us, you would see the same.

She sits here at her desk, this human female, and she writes. She has placed about her neck a crystal she has been building. For a year now, she has been building it. Working with its finer energies, she has with knowing placed it on a gold chain and worn it around her neck, letting it fall over her heart center, while she transmits energies of a higher nature through her body. She was encouraged to do this by those with whom she works, who are "above," so to speak.

She builds the crystal, raising its energies and empowering it with a force greater than it was originally capable of (for it was a gift-shop crystal, manmade, silver). As she assists in empowering this crystal, she raises her own energies because as forces flow through her—her own force, her own generating power from the Earth source—must meet these higher forces and flow in harmony, else she would be destroyed. Her physical point of contact (her body) could not survive the impact and she would shatter. Now what is being asked of her, and what is she asking of herself? Purification, the purifying of the emotional, the mental, and the physical until they can match the purity of the higher calling of energies and flow with them harmoniously. This means she must eat the right foods for her, she must learn to contain the emotions and not let the human self hold sway over the higher self, not even in thought. This means she must control the mind, bending it only to her higher will.

She bends over her desk, pen in hand, crystal around her neck, love-gift from a revered master teacher in her left hand, and writes. The physical body aches, the emotions harbor some resentment, a tinge of anger, and periodically the mind goes astray. Yet she bends and she writes, for she has committed herself, and though the balance is fine at times, though the physical suffers and the mind protests, she continues. She is determined that she can make it. She *will* control the bodily intake, she *will* discipline the mind, and she *will* use the emotions only for the expression of beauty. She is determined.

Say you are building a boat. If, when it is half finished, you should put it overboard, would it float? No, it would sink.

She builds her body, her greater body, and it is half finished. Do not expect it to shine yet. Do not expect it to function properly. It will come together as it nears completion. And in the interim, she works with faith and vision and learns the disciplines that are sensitive to beauty and balance.

The crystal hanging from the chain around her neck, does she build it for herself? No, she builds it for another. She has a man, her counterpart, a mate, and she builds it for him. On this day that we see her, as she placed it around her neck and over her heart (for the chain is fine gold and carries energy too), she felt an overpowering vibration and felt perhaps she might faint. But she placed her slippered feet firmly on the floor, drew strength from the sight of the mountains, took a deep, relaxing breath, and began to write.

It takes courage to build your greater body. It takes determination. It takes wisdom and discipline. It takes right thinking and, above all, it takes faith. Faith in yourself and faith in God's creation. Faith in your connection, your rightful heritage, in God's creation, is needed if you are to participate fully.

If you are to build your greater body and keep your Earth body contact, you must know what you are about and do it properly. We are writing this in the hope that we will be helpful in keeping you in the physical body, so that you might carry out your mission to completion that the world might be a new world and that the sun might become the new Son and harmony reign in all the glades of the world.

You are precious, indeed, to us, those of you who have chosen to work on the Earth plane. You took the hard job, the one with more risk, and we appreciate your loyalty and your steadfastness. Many who were called, who called themselves into duty, have not come forward. We work with a partial crew, yet we must persist and get the work done.

Yes, you are precious indeed, to us, and we have places to go together. Together we will travel the universe and we will see more of God's glory than people have ever beheld or thought possible.

We work nightly together when you come to our bidding and work with us here in the finer ethers . . . and we work daily together when we push as far as we are able into your earth realm and assist you there. Do you feel the coming closeness? Do you sense our closeness more and more? We are not only coming to you, but you are also coming to us! It *does* feel good to be reaching this passage after so many eons of working for it, does it not?

Be patient with yourselves. Your greater bodies are fine works of art and take time to build. With healing and with openness come forward, and we will meet you halfway always and assist and draw you nearer to us, as we all move closer to our Godhead. Is it not a fine work we do? Can you begin to see the world shine with more glory? We can. The light centers were scattered far and wide like seeds in the wind, and they are now beginning to beam in on each other, join hands and voices, and build together. What a few years ago were separate centers are now a network, and the Light grows stronger as the whole face of the globe is dotted with lights that are seeding other lights. We must build this new world together, hand in hand and heart to heart. Are you not glad that we are getting closer? We are. Thank you.

Alam Selam, Go in peace.

"We dedicate ourselves anew to the service of the coming One."

PART THREE

Crystal Light

Lesson 24

BEGINNING ANEW

We now begin a new phase of our study. We have considered that there are many crystals of generous proportions hereabout, and we have decided that, in all likelihood, there is one specific crystal waiting for you. We also have mentioned that you have experienced this crystal before. This member of the mineral kingdom which is your crystal has advanced itself in its years of waiting. Because you trained it in the far distant past, because you planted it here in its present environment, it has advanced itself in its waiting. Knowing that your fondest desire was to unearth it, not knowing that the wait would be as long a wait as it has proven to be, you planted your crystal here and hoped for the day when you might activate it once again. These lands were islands at that time, and a great task force rose en masse behind the back of the government. These jewels of power were secreted suddenly from their standing places of commission and hidden in the mountainous islands that they might be in safekeeping and away from the harm they might effect if they were left in the control of the collapsing government.

It might be helpful to realize that you were a part of the government at that time. A select few became aware of the dangers that were pressing in upon the nation and took it upon themselves to transplant the most important crystals that were movable to a safer place. They chose the islands off the coast. And, as a great diversion was set about by those who knew what they were doing, behind the backs of those who might have stopped them, they flew the crystals to a safer land and planted them in obscurity. It was done within a three-day span and none was the wiser until the whole effect had taken place. Shortly after that, within the week, came the first great earthquake. You were one of these who spirited the crystals away, and you are the same who has your crystal here now. Call it again to you, that you might set up your laboratory and begin your training. It is you who must be trained, and it is you who must train your crystal.

It is known that there are tiny crystals now in full functioning all over the planet. It is known that they contain a vast amount of information in one tiny cell and that they can release this information-energy at will . . . the will of those who control them. Now multiply this and enlarge it, and begin to see huge crystals performing the same function, but doing it on a scale that is as yet unknown, and functioning in such a way as to enhance the beauty of human greatness and the glory of God on Earth. The oneness that must come to humankind if it is to survive is to come partially through the crystals, and those of us who chose to hide ours in the new world now have an obligation to meet the task once again, to train ourselves and see what we can profit, not for ourselves alone, but for humankind.

Did you know that you were going to come full circle? Yes, you did, but you did not know it would be so wide a circle. Did you know that there is a flow of humanity moving full circle with you? There is, and we who are in the finer dimensions at this time have been moving in the flow with you. We are ready to work, and we now dictate this book for transcription that we might be helpful to the cause.

Come forward and search for your crystal. You will find it is waiting for you . . . and has been waiting for some time. It has built itself greater while it has been waiting. It is in fine form and ready to grow. School yourself with this study (and others), and call your crystal to you. It will come as you move about and free yourself for your greater work.

<><><><><>

"We are ancient, and we are new; we span the ages to begin anew."

COMING BACK

If you were to see a stream flowing, and you wished to dip some clear water from this stream, you would move your dipper to the clearest part and dip there, would you not? It is the same with dipping from the memories. If we wish to pull through information about our abilities with crystals, would we not want to return to the most pure part of the memory source and begin our research there? Yes, we would, for in this way we would avoid the contaminants of old that caused us much trouble.

When your crystals, which are here in these mountains now, were deposited by you, they were drawn from, flown from, a troubled time. Yet that time was pure in comparison with some later times, and it was very pure compared with some earlier times. It was a developed time, a time with troubles, yet there was in the air a purity of purpose and a clarity of understanding that was far advanced over that of other times. It was a short-lived period, yet it was potent. It was fraught with dangers, it was unstable, yet it was powerful and clear in its directives.

You who are here now to retrieve your crystals were the leaders in technology. Some of you were in government. You have within your power the ability to pull back to you the information that you need now to reactivate your crystals and use them for a grand purpose . . . to build this new world we are constructing. Forty thousand years ago, you were developing your abilities that apply to the present. Twenty thousand years ago, you removed the crystals which have come back to you now: the very same crystals. They have developed themselves in your absence.

Now you are ready to take them up, meet them at this point of development, and implement their benefits to the planet once again. This time, we must do it correctly. This time we must keep it pure. This time we must dip only from the purest part of the stream. We must take no contaminants with it and build anew.

Twenty thousand years ago, when we built these crystals, it was a time of concentration, and it was a time of highest purity. There-fore, the crystals deposited are the purest energy. They have no contaminants within them. As Atlantis built on itself, it retained abilities that had been useful in the past, and it allowed the new abilities to develop. At one point (and it is the point of which we speak when we removed the hidden crystals), Atlantis had her crown chakra energy open to the cosmic force. As we have said, it was of short duration; however, it was open, ever so slightly, but indeed open. It is at this point that we wish to dip in now with our memory dipper and force an opening, keeping it pure and pro-tected, extract our information, and move forward with it into our present. It will take many talented hands to do this, it will take dedi-cated minds, and our hearts must remain pure and to one pur-pose only, that of serving humankind in peace.

Are you ready to go back? Are you confident that you can return to your original purity . . . that which was with you when you removed the crystals into safekeeping? Your intent was very pure at that time, your ideals high, and your actions justified.

Pick up this energy where you laid it down. Feel its strength again and feel your power of mind behind it. Know that you can enter into the former glory, keep it pure and flower with it for the good of all. It will be a new building this time. It is a new day.

⬦⬦⬦⬦⬦

"We are eternally coming back and moving forward; we are one with the universe; we are one."

LEARNING TO REMEMBER

As you read this book, something is happening to you . . . something that is more than just in the mind. We will explain it to you. As you read this book, it imbues you with a certain flow of energy. Not only do you move with the pattern of the book, the pattern of the words and thoughts, but you move with an outer pattern that surrounds you and changes as you grow. The flow of words is built in such a way, and purposely so, as to enhance your reactions in all of your bodies — mental, emotional, and physical — and to change them in their relationship one to another. Now this is no great secret, that a book changes one in the process of reading. It is no great secret that books are a great instrument for the advancement of a culture. But what we are attempting to share with you now is a new concept to your mind.

As you read, you form an energy field around you. This has always been. This energy field is always formed when there is an act of concentration. It is over and above the usual personal aura. For when you read, you take in a new substance at a rate far more rapid than the usual inflow. It is concentrated. When people first learned to use fire, they had to concentrate on the proper usage of the force they were attempting to control. It is the same now. If you are to learn to control these higher energies with which you wish to work, you must concentrate, and you must learn to use them correctly. To use them carelessly is like playing with fire. In reading this book, you are being prepared, *or preparing yourself*, to handle the new energy field that is forming about you. This book is written in such a way, the flow of words are built in such a way, as to cause within you a change. Now we say within you, and we are speaking about your greater body . . . building your greater body. We have spoken about the crystal that hangs on a golden chain about the neck of the transcriber, the scribe, the channel. We have said that *it* is being imbued with a certain ability, a certain force power. It is the same as with you. It is as if you, too, had a crystal hanging from your neck, and around your heart center there revolves a certain energy that is building as you read, and it is sharpening your responses in your memory. We build our greater bodies finer if we are to do the work we have promised.

Do you feel the changes within you? Do you realize that you respond to a book from more than one level? Are you aware that as you respond more fully, you build your greater body, your finer bodies, to a higher completion than before? This book is written, dictated if you will, in such a manner that it enhances this ability within you. A certain flow of the words in a certain paragraph can be built in such a way as to help you think of yourself more freely and help you open to your greater self. As you flow with this energy, as you read, you grow . . . not only in your intellectual self, but in your spiritual self.

This book has been called a primer. It has been called basic, a beginning textbook, a workbook for beginners. It is indeed that, for as you read, you are beginning to get back in touch with that which you lost, something immeasurably precious to you. In this memory coming back, there will be certain powers enhanced and these powers are what you will use with your new body.

When all the bodies are integrated, we call this the greater body. It is to your present knowledge of yourself as your whole physical self is to one hair on your head or one portion of your tiniest fingernail. You are great indeed, and little do you know, as yet, what abilities you have with which to build this new world.

As you read this book, you grow. You flow in an energy field that is building strength from each new word you read. Not that the words are new to you, or necessarily the ideas, but you join with thousands of other minds who are reading the same material, and you build a new, strong aura that is at the same time part of you and part of the All.

Do you see this? Do you believe this? You do not need to see it or believe it. It is happening. Because there is a new language beginning, because we have initiated ourselves into a new and glorious project, there is about us a new energy. Deprived of this energy for some time now, we are ravenous for it. The thought of it instills within us a longing that will not be quiet. This new energy about us needs nourishment on which to feed. If it does not receive the nourishment, it dissipates, and when we feel it waning, we hurry to make adjustments so it will reinstate itself around us. This is all done in the higher mind and knowing, and sometimes the human self wonders what the frantic activity is all about and berates itself for strange behavior.

You went to a party. It was a gathering where those who attended were to eat, enjoy one another's company, share stories, play some music for one another, and in general be in the moment, which was to be made pleasant and away from the workaday world. It was for relaxing and for the benefit of the *body-mind-spirit*.

At this gathering, you began to feel a pressure to which you were unaccustomed. It persisted until you were unable to contain your thoughts about it. You expressed in words your concern about your condition to your friend beside you, and to your surprise and comfort, your friend had the same concern about herself. She was feeling the pressure, too. You looked about you, and you began to perceive that there were others in the room who felt the same way. Something new was happening, not definable, yet constantly it plagued their waking and sleeping and was intensifying. Do you remember us speaking of the longing heart? It is the same thing, yet some feel it more keenly in the mind than in the heart.

There is about you a new energy. To speak of this new energy, you must develop a new language. You are experiencing an awareness of this new energy field. It is often sensed as pressure, an uneasy feeling that something must be done. As a little child fumbles with his first few words of expression, you attempt to express this newness to others, and you find they understand and are experiencing the same difficulty. So as you express yourself, choose new thought patterns and use new words. Allow the new language to become. Let us try it now in an exercise:

Will you wind with me through one of the old streets of Atlantis and see what we might find that would be helpful to the filling out of our memory? We have come down some rough-hewn stairs of stone; we are in an old part of the city. There are beggars about, but they are not destitute. They simply earn their living by asking. It has always been so. We move forward along the street, the two of us, and we come to a sector where the street widens into a square. The sunlight falls more easily here, and there are even plantings, a few trees, hanging flowers from some window ledges, and some hedges. It was the glory of the old city to work its life forms of the plant world into an integral containment of the energy force of each building. We turn and go into an offset doorway that is slightly removed from the square down the side of one tall building. Are you beginning to remember?

We go up a flight of stairs and meet our friend, the one with whom we had an appointment. He is in a room flooded with light. Yes, the sun comes in the eastern windows, yet there is a lightness to the room beyond that which the sun is producing. Our friend greets us with a smile and a clasp on each of our shoulders. We sit at a table on which he has many drawings. We study these drawings for several hours while a gentle animal being brings us warm fluid to drink in wooden containers.

Suddenly, in our vision (because we cannot hear the language), our friend rises. Placing a marker on one of the large sheets of paper to hold the place, he turns and opens two wide panels behind us. We enter into a different room, which is flooded with pink light, and we sit to eat. There are no outside windows in this room, but there is a panel of light coming from the ceiling, and it bathes us in a feeling of love. The eating is very pleasant. No flesh is consumed, yet there is an abundance of root vegetables and nuts that make us realize it is the main meal of the day. Looking down at your clothes, you see leather and you see soft wool; the inner garments are of a fine linen texture. Are you beginning to remember?

On rising from the table, we pass through a corridor, passing by some shut panels that must contain private space for study or sleep, and we emerge onto an enclosed deck on the side of the building. Here we look at plants, some in bloom and some without flower, but with broad leaves. We inspect these long leaves carefully and then walk back to our drawing board and the papers and studying instruments.

In old Atlantis, there was much enthusiasm for improving the way of life. There was much enthusiasm for using the plant kingdom to its very highest form of dedication. Here we have seen the emergence of a new product, a plant cultivated through the use of lights and crystals that was eventually to be put to much use for the benefit of the populace. You did not see any crystals? You each carried one in your pocket. There were some in the eastern window above the panel, and there were many implanted in the pink ceiling panel of light. On the enclosed deck, the star forms in the translucent ceiling were embedments of crystals. They had become of common usage for those of the educators and those who were employed to apply the science of the mind to practical living. Crystals were at the budding stage at this time, yet they were used correctly with much effectiveness.

Lean back in your chair now, close your eyes. Really do it. Take the time. Again, bring yourself through these few scenes we have just witnessed. Add to them. See things you did not see through our eyes, and . . . remember. You can remember as well as the one next to you, and the pressure you feel in your aura at times is your memories wanting to come back and your future job wanting to come to you. It is your *superconsciousness*, your expanded awareness speaking to you. It is the you-that-is-to-be calling to the you-now, wanting to join hands and work. Lean back, close your eyes, and remember. Allow. Allow the future to come flooding in on the past, and make it now, the ever-present, eternal now.

⬦⬦⬦⬦⬦

"We are learning to remember."

REMEMBERING CLEARLY

Now there is one among us, namely the transcriber of this material, who has been trained to remember more clearly. You too can remember this clearly, but in actuality the remembering will come as a side effect of your ability to purify your purpose and your intent. When your actions are pure, you have no reason to forget, for your thoughts carry through the forever where you can balance and adjust and accept who you are. Make worthy your own actions, and you will remember well. The more pure you are, the more clearly you remember.

Let us now remember together. As a string of pearls, you wove your lives in old Atlantis. One after another time, you came in to do your work there. It was for your own training and for the benefit of the world that you entered. You were wont to do it well, so you specialized, and studied hard and long in your training. Over many lifetimes, you wove a pattern of completion for your soul, and you dared not forsake your promise that you would build a better world. You worked diligently and trained yourself well. Now we are ready to pick up on that training and see that we do it well this time, for the period of purification of the facts draws near to a close, and we are ready to begin.

We can first deal with the fact that crystals were a long time coming to their maturity in old Atlantis. At first, they were used as toys, or stones to carry, as little goodies that one could pocket and have around, because they were pleasant to hold, to see, to give as gifts. Then, as the minds began to sense the inner knowledge of the crystals, there began to blossom in some of the creative minds the potential of the inner nature of the energy patterns of the crystals ... and little experiments were set up to watch the flow of energy, the sensitive patterns of light that would flow from the crystals as they were used in certain ways. Following that came the knowledge that they actually might generate power that could be used in utilitarian ways. This took place over a period of hundreds of years.

There were specific times for breakthroughs, when the understanding and the employment of the crystal would take a leap. So we begin with the toy, with the pleasant object to have about, and we move forward step by step by step in the understanding of the crystal until there is a huge crystal in the center of the city, in the bowels of a building, where it is activated through an empowering of its structure, pulling in the rays of the daytime sun and the nighttime moon.

This crystal was a forerunner of the "great" crystal that is often remembered. This crystal of which we speak now is in obscurity. This crystal in its color was as a glass with smoke in it, smoky quartz. It was mined from a hillside in Atlantis. It was an earthbound crystal, one that had been formed by the planes of the planet Earth. It was not activated to send radiation out to the populace. It was for schooling only, for the instruction of those who were learning to employ the use of crystals. It was in the experimental stage. We speak of it, we bring it back to memory, we bring it back to conscious acknowledgment, because it was at this time that many were schooled with this crystal, and there is a parallel here to your day.

They proceeded cautiously in that day for two reasons. One, their own mental ability was limited, and to comprehend some of the abstracts that the crystal was lending to them stressed the mind beyond the present ability, and there had to be the drawing back for assimilation and growth. The second reason was that there was an innate knowledge, that here was a source of power that might be too powerful for containment by the human mind, that the human mind might not be disciplined enough.

Through the use of the mind in the human being in conjunction with the crystal, the energies of the moon, for example, could be enticed to draw a vibration in the face of the crystal that would permeate its interior and set up a reservoir, a holding pattern, so that this might be built upon itself night after night until there would eventually be within the crystal itself a pool, a bank of energy, that would be the healing energy of the moon. This was done by the mind, the active mind pulling the cool vibrations from the moon and allowing them to carve a pattern on the face of the crystal, the surface of the crystal, as the moonlight fell upon it. Eventually, a few hundred years later, people would learn at the same time to implant their own information with the inflow of the energy so that there would be a pool not only of healing energy from the moon, but also correct thinking, thoughts, that could flow forth at the appropriate time of instruction. These were to be released so that there would be the coupling of the healing with correct thoughts. It was as if you were to take a modern dictaphone recording and release it at an appropriate time so that the message, the energy, and the vibration would be released for a specific purpose at a correct time for the healing of an individual. Now, once it was placed, it would be like a deep freeze. It would be information that could not be tampered with, except one had the key to unlocking the crystal. It would be unchanging, and it would not wane in its ability or its energy or its power. The battery would not lose energy for a long, long time. For a period of millions of years, it would not lose its energy once it was set.

The key to unlocking the crystal was purity in heart, and the resonance of the voice pattern, and the ability to activate the heart energy with the voice pattern. At times, to bring in the energy of the other energy centers of the physical structure of the person who was the keeper of the crystal was necessary to unlock the power.

There were students who were trained, and the key to the crystal was passed on to one individual. It was a careful linking, a cautious training and a quiet matter. Also in this crystal, the smoky quartz crystal of which we have spoken, there were different compartments for the sake of the training and learning of different experimenters. This is not the usual pattern of crystals. A crystal is really abused if it has more than one master. This crystal was abused. It was used by many for their research work, but it was well used with good intent. It would have been more pleasant for the crystal itself, however, if it had had one master. In this way, it would have had the opportunity to develop its own centeredness, its own sources of energy in a systematic, correct, growth pattern. As it was, it was used for knowledge gained, for learning. It was well used with good intent, but it is not an example of a centered crystal.

The crystal is the king of the mineral kingdom. It has itself projecting in a way toward its own reaching for its own Christ consciousness. It has all of its molecular structure aligned toward the purification of its purpose. It is a perfect container for crystallized energy of any sort that might want to be implanted within it.

⬦⬦⬦⬦⬦

"We are remembering clearly."

IN SEARCH OF THE GREAT CRYSTAL

People have for some time now, at one level or another, been desirous of a haven, a "heaven on earth," where they might express themselves more fully as the great beings they are. They have often drawn pictures for themselves of what this haven might be like. In this wishing, they have lingered in their memory sometimes in places where they remember an "almost haven," where they almost made it.

Often in their minds as they search, a time looms large when there was a great crystal, a huge obelisk that shone in the sun in a lovely garden, and it was the pride of many. Later, the memories cloud, and the crystal seems to have been taken into the hands of the few and hidden out of sight for unwise use and not for the benefit of all. Where is this great crystal now? Is it still on the face of the Earth? Is it still operable? Time will tell . . . for once we have come full circle, we draw nearer to that which we accomplished before, and we understand more fully how we may draw on the past to fill out the present and draw our dreams into the future.

We live to learn. We do not live the past, but we learn from the past. There have been some times so potent, so full of reward for our efforts that we dare not neglect them when we build for the coming day. For would we cast out that which is valuable when we begin to compile a beauteous composite of events and understandings, or would we instead stand on our toes and peek over the years and collect that which is valuable and precious and use it to our cause?

We have here a memory so precious that it calls us back time and time again to review it. We bring it to the present in the form of longing. We school ourselves with its memory, and we long for its visible presence in the present. It will come. It will surface when we have prepared the ground. When we have created a setting suitable in our own hearts and in our environment, it will come forward, and greater than it even, and we must abide in harmony. Many factors coming together for one central cause, for one united purpose, we will attain our goal of the haven, where we can create in peace and bless our beloved planet with many benefits and love flowering in the hearts of all.

But first we must start small and grow toward our understanding of our own potential and our own needs to fulfill that potential: Step by step is the process of fulfillment, and in this way do we prove our own worth and our own ability. The huge crystal that we had built ourselves toward was one that even today we are not ready for, for you see we come about the terms in life in circuitous ways, and we prepare ourselves well, yet we miss the mark if we do not come face to face with ourselves fully and find ourselves flawless. So again we come full circle and challenge ourselves to the task of purity, of purity of purpose, and as we move forward, we see more attention being paid to the possible use of crystals to enhance the life quality of the populace . . . so let us study.

The different colors of crystals designate the different vibrations. The ability of people to perceive these different vibrations and the different qualities designated by the different colors because of the different vibrations is soon to come. It might help to understand that whereas one crystal would sing at a high pitch, another might resonate at a lower tone, each for its own individual reason. When we speak about crystals, it is difficult to speak of the Earth tones and the Earth vibrations only, because a crystal works with light and light is an other-than-Earth vibration. Light is a universal vibration, and it penetrates into the Earth vibration and mingles with it and vibrates with it, but does not make itself of the Earth. So when we speak of the colors of crystals—and we might speak of a blue crystal, or a red, or a green—we would be speaking partly of the Earth substance that holds the mineral together. We would also be speaking of light and the way that light interacts with the mineral in order to make the color. So we are not speaking of just Earth colors, we are also speaking of light.

We would mention to you the energy centers of the physical human body. We would say we have been taught that the root energy resonates with a red vibration. Then, as you go up the scale, you pass through the orange, you move into the yellow, the seat of the soul, then you move up into the green vibration, then into the blue, and the different shades of blue, then you move into the violet, and then into the ultraviolet. So if you would take a crystal and you would see it as a deep blue crystal, a cobalt blue, you would ask, where do we place this on this diagram of the human energy centers? Our explanation is that you would not place it there, because they do not coincide. There is a need to let go of the former understanding, the former prejudices, and former schooling of the colors and their vibratory rates in relationship to the ladder towards the Christ consciousness.

Crystals have the embodiment of the mineral kingdom, but they circulate light within them, and they reflect a certain aspect of their environment and their nurturing since their conception. Their scale of vibratory rate has more to do with their density, and their transparent or translucent qualities than it does with their specific color. So we would picture a golden crystal that is what one might call topaz, and it is very transparent. We can see the light piercing through it as we turn it and look in it. Then you have again another topaz crystal that is less clear, more milky in quality; the light does not reflect through it as easily. You would understand that in most circumstances, that one which is more clear, that the light can penetrate through more easily, is of a higher vibration. So you take an aquamarine crystal that is a light quality, one that the light can pierce through easily. You can see the reflections and the refractions of the light passing through it quickly. Then, you hold up a deeper blue crystal, and it is of a slower vibration than that one which the light can pass through quickly.

Now in this evaluation, do not assume that the higher frequency is the better for the use, because it all depends upon the use. We are only speaking here of the vibratory rate of the crystals. You will come to find that those that hold a lower vibration might be more useful than those who hold the higher vibration, depending upon the use that you wish to put them to.

In this new day, the clarity or the vibratory rate of a crystal will have nothing to do with its value. However, it will help in the understanding of the usages to know that the clearer it is, the higher its vibration; and those that are more cloudy resonate to a slower vibration . . . and that the frequency often determines the usage.

In the great crystal, we had a structure that could lower or raise its own vibration according to the need. As we work to clear ourselves, and as we grow nearer to that which we understand is to be, we will activate within ourselves control over our own vibrations. Our own thought patterns will become more controlled and constructive. We will foster within ourselves a willingness to work with enlightened substances correctly. We will draw to us that which we need to build our new day, and our gardens will shine with flowers and crystals alike, each bringing its quality for the healing of all.

⬦⬦⬦⬦⬦

"Searching for the great crystal, we find it within."

Lesson 29

TIME TO TAKE STOCK

Each one of us is unique in our own way. There are no two dewdrops or snowflakes alike. In this universe, the vast unexplored and unending expanse that it is, there are no two souls alike. Do you realize the unbelievable majesty of this? If the human mind were capable of comprehending this fact, this reality, it would be indeed the Great Mind.

In the human form, we can but feel the greatness. We cannot comprehend it fully. But we can work with what we know, and we can feel with our whole being how that which is, is extraordinary to the greatest degree, and that we are a part of it, a *necessary* part of it, that we are essential and unique and beautiful.

As we take stock of how far we have come and where we are going, let us always remember that we are beautiful. As we face trials that are for our pruning and our better growth, let us not lose sight of the fact that we have been conceived in beauty, that we grow in beauty, and that we produce beauty around us.

By this standard, what is the definition of beauty? Surely that which we see is often not beautiful! We have scarred the face of the planet with that which would erase the security of its balance and its internal structure. We have not been kind to our neighbors. We have often profited much at the expense of others. We have let ourselves go in wanton ways and not answered to justice. Have we been so wayward and yet you would call us beautiful? To say that we produce beauty when all about us we can see that which brings us to shame seems irresponsible.

In order to evaluate correctly that which is our whole being, we must look beyond that which we see close by, we must expand our vision and comprehend the relationship of the parts one to another. Our Earth selves are but a small part of our life force. We are minute in our Earth touching compared to our selves that extend into God's universe. If you were to look at a great being shining with light, and you were to notice a blemish on one great toenail, would you call that being of light beautiful or unbeautiful?

Look at your greater selves. Extend your vision beyond the clouds. Look to heaven and the part of you that resides there. Then revolve around the compass of time and see your many other aspects. What do you see? Do not tie yourself down to the Earth memories. Expand your horizons, push them out until you begin to be flooded with your greatness. Feel your essence, your ethers, and your central awareness comprehending that which you are. Do you sense that the universe is great? Do you get a glimpse of the intricate patterns, no two alike? Do you begin to see the Light shining through each structure? Do you feel the touch and hear the music? With all your senses, allow yourself to flow into your knowing of the universe. Then turn about and look at the little leaf in the forest with the flower above it, and see the same structure. You are beautiful, oh human child, and you are a part of the planet Earth, and your greater self extends into the universe, and it is ready to come home.

The Earth does not have to be a decrepit place where you learn your lessons in drudgery. It can be a fine school shining with light and full of lessons that train with love, lessons that flow into one another, as the stream flows into the river, and the river flows into the ocean. It is only that you see the distressing side of the detail, because you have committed yourself to correct it. *That* causes the imbalance in your vision. If you will permit yourself to take stock correctly, you will see a great light being who has committed a portion of himself to creating a New World that is yet unfinished. As he works, he deals with that at hand which is yet to be proven. He concentrates on this, because it is the raw material of the substance with which he works. He wishes to create into a finished product that which is unfinished. When something is unfinished, it does not flow with the whole. It has not been hooked up to the greater machine, because it is not finished in itself yet; it is not ready "to go." Once it is completed, once it has found its own completeness, then it can become a part of the whole and flow fully in the giving and receiving. Then, keeping itself fully nourished, it becomes one with the Whole.

We have in part, when we work with crystals, an example of a mechanism that is a unit within itself, yet it is of necessity a part of another for its completion. We are all appendages of one another, and we all form a whole. Yet in each individual part, in each individual human being, is a whole unit in itself. It is a part of the structure of this universe, this complex arrangement, and it is well that we understand it fully, at a very deep level, if we are to work with the power source of crystals.

Nothing that we do affects only us. We can make no choice, no decision is made even, that does not affect many. Sometimes we think we can "get away with something." We think we can crawl off by ourselves and do something that is to our temporary liking, and we will affect no one; we will be a unit by ourselves. It is not possible . . . and the more you grow on the scale of understanding, the more you realize that this is not possible.

To acknowledge that you are one with the universe and that all you produce by your own actions affects every other living thing is awe inspiring, to say the least. It makes you want to not move. On the other hand, it might make you want to produce in quantity. For if you love and you love so completely that you want to chance reaching out, even making mistakes, in order to build, then you have tapped that fountain within yourself that wants to flow with the all.

Take heart. There are many like you who have reached their stage of completion where they too wish to serve and serve abundantly. As you join hands and do the work about you that you see needs to be completed, there will come a strengthening of the spirit within, and much will come forward to be of assistance.

It is a matter of beginning where you are now, taking stock, and continuing with what must be done in this moment to lead you to the place where you can free yourself to be in the place of greatest service. It must all be done in love . . . every step following every other step in love. If you find you have taken a step in anger or malice, you must return and take that step over in love, and that slows down the progress considerably.

So move forward with your mission. Let this book inspire you to grow, to search for your crystal consciousness with your inner nature, and to attain that height where you will be clear to work with purity and with knowledge, knowing full well that as you do so, you become God incarnate, and you follow in the steps of the one who taught love more perfectly than ever before.

Move with your knowing. Perfect your day each day. Reward yourself with pleasant memories as you fall asleep at night, and cast away that which you choose to have no part of yourself contain. It is a pleasant day that harbors only love, and you can produce this for yourself and those in your environment. You have this within your power. Your creative ability includes this pattern for this masterpiece. Attempt, this day, and you will achieve.

⬦⬦⬦⬦⬦

"Taking stock, we find that we can serve abundantly and wisely."

THE MAGNIFICENT JOURNEY

"What about specifics?" you ask. "What about the technical material?" "When are we going to get down to more specifics?" We will. You will. We understand your frustration. But we would have you know that it was exactly that impatience that lead you into trouble before. "When the student is ready, the teacher appears." You are now being schooled in purity. You are being more than schooled . . . you are being healed. As you read this book, healing is coming to you. Do you feel it? We are composing the words, the thoughts, the sentences in such a way as to allow them to be as healing to you as possible. "New-speak" was spoken of in George Orwell's insightful book *1984*. This is the new-speak. Only this time, we have come further than he thought we would. We have enlightened ourselves more than he predicted . . . by far. We have put on new garments, have cast off the old, and we are ready to advance. We have passed through the door of escape that no one passed through in Orwell's book, and we are ready to train ourselves for the new.

Do you remember being admonished, "Don't say anything, if you can't say something good"? Are you aware of what we have said when we speak of the voice tones controlling the key that unlocks the crystals? Do you realize that much has been said about your being able to comprehend the intricacies of the vibrations and handle them correctly? Well, you begin here. Right here in this book, while you study, you are being guided to purify yourself from the inside out until you might be pure enough, sincere enough, clear enough, that you might be worthy to serve humankind.

As you move into higher vibrations in your functioning, your deeds, thoughts, and activities pertaining to self must come clear and be for a good purpose only. No one can travel in the higher energy and forsake their birthright of purity without disastrous results. Within one being, the energies of love and devotion and the energies of contempt and remorse cannot abide simultaneously for long without causing a disharmony that would fracture the wholeness of the being. If you wish to be whole and you desire to continue your work in the Light, you must lift yourself into love action. Every moment you must abide in love and kindness. "Impossible," you say, "No being has done it yet!" Are you building a new world, and is that new world to be one of Light? Then it must be inhabited by beings of Light. Prepare yourself. You have no cause to doubt that you can make it. You have started on the right track. You have answered to the desire within you. You have spoken the first few words and felt the first few pullings that cause you to know you have a destiny and a mission. So now you set about the task of preparing yourself, and like a trainer preparing himself for competition, you school yourself in all your parts until you are ready for your job.

With application comes the working out of the specifics. If we were to give you the key now, you would use it incorrectly or you might just hold it and stare. You are not ready. Prepare yourself, and you will see the key and the specifics coming to you, many of them through your own inner knowing. You can see that until you know, until you have discovered and have worked out specifics, there is little use to attempt to understand, because until one is applying them, one cannot have reason for the details. You must purify first.

Acquaint yourself with crystals . . . become acquainted with them and continue to clear your consciousness. Continue to make yourself of a higher nature and more of a being of light. There is to come to the planet a great day when all will be more visibly beautiful through and through. The planet will still be a school, a teaching planet, but it will be of a much gentler, much kinder nature. Crystals are to play their part and to give their all, so to speak, in the turning of this transformation.

Do you realize that as we speak and you read, you are being healed? Do you realize all this could be said more cryptically, and the information would spill out, but it would not fit with your vibration? Bathe yourself in your new knowing. Do not rush. What is the sense of taking a journey through beautiful territory, if you rush? One might as well be wrapped in a package and sent in the mail, if one does not plan to gaze long out the windows from time to time and enjoy the view. One might even back up, stop, and absorb nourishment from one special view, one special comprehension, if one wishes. We will get there . . . but first we must grow in stature and fit ourselves for the job.

As we grow closer to the time when we will learn to beautify our environment and work in harmony with the all that is the total content of the planet Earth vibration (working in harmony with each other factor of this marvelous life being, the Earth), then the crystals will have their fulfillment, their flowering into their greater glory in the service of generating power for the planet to function as a whole. For the beings walking the face of the planet to have their needs met, which requires empowerment by rigid centers of energy or condensed centers of energy, is their dedication. The mineral kingdom wishes to come forward to work in a more developed way with this, and to provide this service as a part of their pattern of their growth. The crystals, as we have said, are the outstanding exponents of the mineral kingdom that raise the rest of their fellow beings forward with the raising of their own highest consciousness. They are willing, eager, to serve in this capacity. They bring themselves forward to work with people.

So as we come to the end of our magnificent journey, as the train, the generating force, slows done, let us gaze out the window hard and long. Let us begin to see that we are chosen, that we have chosen ourselves, to do a great job. As we pick up our luggage and our briefcase and step out onto the platform, let us take a deep breath and fill ourselves with freshness, for this is rarified air we breathe, and it makes us flow with light. We have stepped out onto the platform of the higher ethers, and we consider ourselves still human . . . yet we are divine in nature, for we are ready to serve in whatever capacity we must to bring our beloved planet and the inhabitants on it into the realm of the eternal and glorious, where songs are sung without ceasing, and knowledge is given freely for the healing of all.

⟨⟩⟨⟩⟨⟩⟨⟩

"We are on a magnificent journey of which there is no end and no beginning."

THE POINT IN THREE

 We will investigate our attitude more thoroughly, and in order to do so, let us move forward to the time when the great crystal was in operation. The employment of the great crystal, and the empowering of its ability, came when Atlantis had built itself into an empire that was unequaled in power anywhere else on the planet. This civilization had advanced itself rapidly over the years until it had built up a mecca heard about at firesides around the world, but experienced only by those few souls who chose to live there at that time. As these souls rejuvenated themselves in the higher spheres and returned consistently to the same drawing boards, in this great city, a well of information formed that pinpointed around the activation of a mineralized crystal of vast size and powerful potential. Built up over a period of time, the information proved to be too intricate and delicate in its offerings for human beings to handle, for they had not raised their generosity toward their kind sufficently to meet its moral obligations.

What is called the great crystal is a memory so difficult for so many that it is yet shrouded in mystery, for human beings burnt their consciousness with their employment of the great crystal . . . so that they, as yet, wish to remember only incorrectly that which there is to recall. There are many closed doors, and many people peep through the keyholes wishing for glimpses, at the same time knowing that they are not ready to see and see fully. Many of the reports are in actuality of other crystals, and the great crystal in many aspects still lies quite hidden. If you were to recall at this time detailed accounts of your interactions with the great crystal, you would so complicate your thinking and your life that you would not make a straight path of clearing the way toward another time when you might search within your heart for the ability to deal with such great power and such great potential.

For there to be clarity in your mind about the memories of the great crystal, there must be a cleansing of the heart and a purification of the purpose, a purification of your motives. There are many myths. There are many memories . . . some true memories, but they are so surrounded with and interposed with myths that there is at this time no substantial amount of clarity. It is well, really, that you not remove the veil until you are strong enough. You must be willing to clear yourself if you are to remember. It is a path of progression. It is a step-by-step process. As you contact once again the small crystals and work with them (the kind you can carry in your pocket or around your neck), as you clear yourself, call to yourself for more purity, for more love in your interactions with other beings, then you will be closer to the time when you can make the planet beautiful and help the mineral kingdom activate its full potential.

If you were to recall with absolute certainty, completeness and clarity a previous time when you had many assets and abilities that you have lost in your relationship with a specific other kingdom, as the mineral kingdom; if you were to recall it abruptly and completely, it would do you no benefit, because you must *walk* your way towards that recall, clearing out of the way as you go those scatterings that you caused yourself by closing yourself off from your greater love. It is as if a cloud cover came over right when the sun was most golden. The cloud cover must not be removed too quickly, else one might see great ugliness that you would prefer not to see. You might first like to work under the cloud cover, cleaning up, and then when it is clean enough, the cloud cover will move aside, the golden sun can pour down its beauty, and then all will be more pleasant to behold, and the way will be open for action. It must be realized that we have here a building anew, yet as we build we abstract that which was and decipher it as part to part, and as a jigsaw puzzle, place it together again. We place in the spaces of some of the missing pieces those things that we have invented since the original gain, and we have a new structure. Is this clear?

In this primer, we give to you a benefit you have not requested. With your conscious mind, you have not made the bid. Albeit you chose the pattern, the way still remains dim, and you linger in your memories not quite certain that this which you produce dates back to the right connection. You do not need to date it back, you only need to purify, and the whole picture will come clear to you. The pieces will fit together fine, and you will be able to fill in the parts requested by others. They, too, will supplement your findings and supply your needs. In this way, and this way *only*, will it be accomplished. This is the safety switch that we have built for each other.

There is no need to see any information as foreign, if we are to complete this task. Everyone will be necessary to pull their part. No one nation has the hoist that will raise the glory of the potential again. Each nation has a crew line, and the lifting, the rising, will come as we carry out our given duties and bring forward our offerings to the new day.

As the sun begins to come through the cloud cover, realize there is no need to look at too much ugliness. We have looked at enough. There is only a need to look at enough to know where it is to be able to clean it up. You do not need to look at the whole thing, you only need to look at your individual part and to follow *your* knowledge of your own cleansing and your own correction.

Not only will nations need to pull together, but individuals will need to work together in a way that they have not known before. There will be no bartering for the best for oneself, but all will be brought to the fore for the good of many, and each component will be necessary to fill out the grid that will complete the system enough to have it work for all. No part will be able to function by itself.

The first dawning will come when all begin to see that in series of threes, things are now beginning to be accomplished. It is the network forming. As in the age of two, it took only two parts to make a whole, now in the age of three, it takes three parts to generate the energy necessary to ignite the spark that creates. If you were to take three people, each working his or her part and each producing on his or her own that which was necessary for his or her countenance extended, his or her completion, and you were to place them together, you would see a new energy created that would be a balance in itself. It would be as a new being, for it would generate that which was above and beyond the combination of the three parts.

Let us here return to the site of our blue crystal as an example. The individuals that find themselves here at this site now number three. It is the beginning. At this time, there is an awareness of the crystals, but the unearthing of them is yet to come. They are as a triad, these individuals. They have placed themselves such in relationship to one another, as to assist each other in the cleansing. This extends itself in their individual corrections, and in their corrections as a unit of energy together as a triad force.

Now, there are three crystals, and there are three individuals schooling themselves in the energy of the crystal sight. The potential is that each individual, as he or she births cheer and hope, of himself will draw nearer to his or her own crystal to employ.

The blue crystal lies dormant. Singing to itself, it awaits the day of its reconstruction. Near it are two other components of the crystalline energy that are to someday work in force with it. The same as the human beings, the crystals will align themselves with one another until they have come to their completion in one another, and they will then come into an understanding of their power and of their generative force for good on this planet. The same again with the three human beings. As they align themselves with one another in harmony, they will feel their greatness and their mastery over themselves much more keenly than before, and they will know that to work together in coopera- tive, peaceful effort one with another as a unit of three will bring much better results in this age than could one or even the unit of two.

For we have come to the parting of the individual into separate energies in your one part where you balance yourself more com- pletely in conjunction with two other neighbors and complete the task jointly with them as your coworkers and counterparts. It is the age of the triad, and you will see functioning now the units of three in all things. It is a supplementary energy over the two, and is beyond it in its ability to create. As a molecule reaches out for the furthering of its space and the diminishing of its self- centeredness it vibrates more rapidly and extends the swaying effect of its own generative energy into wider and wider circles. The same with the human centering of energy, as you reach out and extend your own awareness beyond your own self- centeredness, you will find in that of your brother that which is part of you, and you will choose to erase the lines of separateness and enfold your brother in an extension of yourself, and their energies will blend. Albeit the human form will stay the same, the etheric body will be transformed, and there will be light cen- ters with three points operating over the face of the land, and the rainbow hues of our creation will shine more clearly.

◁▷◁▷◁▷◁▷

"We are each a point of Light reflected in all: every prism, every facet, every face."

THE SONG OF THE CRYSTALS

You have heard of the whales' song, how they sing to one of their brothers or sisters at a greater distance, how when the song is carried through the vibration of the water, also love and energy and nourishment for one another is carried. Think of the whales' song, how elusive it is, and how it took people a long time to appreciate its beauty, its power, its fullness. The crystals sing the same kind of song to one another over the whole face of the Earth.

The mineral kingdom is as the whale family when they come to communicate with one another. They sing this song in their own individual tone vibrations to one another. They are schooled, more so than people, in working with energy patterns with one another. Because they are the mineral kingdom does not mean that they do not excel, in their own way, in some things much over human ability. In their own uniqueness, their own specialties, the things that they have allowed themselves to excel in, they can do better than human beings. Else why would people employ them to do something that they cannot do? When these crystals speak to each other over the surface of the Earth, they form a network, a powerful design of energy. It is a strong, integrated, cosmic energy. They will have ability to use this, and you will be able to employ them to serve your cause, when you have brought yourself into your own individual beauty, so that you deserve their closeness and their service.

The three crystals that we have spoken of include the rays of cobalt blue, golden yellow, and ruby red. They bathe themselves during their waiting period in patience and serenity. They call to one another for support, and they send out songs to that human whom they feel is nearest to them in vibration and cause. They are of themselves a total soul. They work together as a triad in complete harmony with one another. They are in communication with each other at all times. You would see it as an elongated communication, for maybe one word, and certainly one sentence, might take two thousand years to complete. This is their language . . . their vibration . . . their life.

Let us follow the pattern of individuals in their relationship to their crystal for our instruction. As we have said, each crystal points its energy toward a certain human being. The ruby crystal, for instance, centers its energy on certain individuals in the eventuality that they choose to take as part of their instruction and part of their service to the planet, working in conjunction with a crystal. These individuals have the ability, the potential, the past history to do so. They only need to choose once again to dedicate themselves in this manner. Their vibration is in relationship to the ruby as no other. They can match oscillations and the changes within the ruby crystal better than most of those about them. They have put themselves in the periphery of the crystal's aura. They have drawn near enough in their consciousness (and often even in their physical whereabouts) to be exchanging energy and thought patterns with the crystal. They begin to feel its energy "within their bones" and often frequent the area where the crystal lies hidden without knowing why they do so. They begin to devote time in thought to moving to the site, and they attempt to purchase the land, or at least to have easy accessibility to it. In their higher mind, they hear the calling of the song. They can leave the thought for weeks, but they surprise themselves by seeing plans they did not see before and acting on them not fully knowing why.

It might be mentioned here that you do not need to picture your full creative time being spent working only with crystals.

This is a crystal primer, so we concentrate on this aspect. However, you need to understand that once you have schooled yourself in closeness to a crystal and have taken up your position as the one who has the key to a specific crystal, then you have a lock-box of reserve energy that you can tap at any time. You can leave this energy source at any time, as long as you do it just service. If you do not leave it inert, it will still respond to you on your return and be yours to school yourself with and to use for the benefit of humankind. If you were to abandon it and leave it inert for too long a time, another would be drawn near and come into relationship with it and use it. It would form a new key, for the old key would have been thrown away, and the lock sealed. Out of disuse, it would have evaporated its formula and sealed over the equation. As long as a crystal is being employed, as long as it is being given an opportunity to use itself and to grow in its own pattern, then it will attach itself to that one and be dedicated and faithful in that service to that one person.

The ruby crystal, the golden crystal, and the blue crystal each has its service to perform, and at this time of writing have attached themselves to individuals and are serving in their own way. In the near future, the service will be more apparent, more acknowledgeable, and will surface (literally) so that all might have more comprehension of it. Let us explain: The absence of one in a triad immediately begins to draw within its structure another to replace the one missing, because as a cell cannot exist healthily without all of its functioning parts, a triad cannot exist healthily without all of its active parts. If there is a withdrawing with intent not to return, then immediately somewhere in the universe another energy of like nature begins to draw into that space that has been left empty. It is the same with the crystal. If a crystal wishes to activate itself in the service of humankind, it has to channel its energy through a specific human being. If that human being forms a relationship with the crystal, it will attach itself to that one and be faithful and dutiful in its service through that one. If that human being detaches himself and loses interest and does not set his mental structure towards the crystal continually, then that crystal will immediately send its song out to someone else. It will shift and search and call for another aspirant to come to begin to work with it.

There can be times when a crystal will send its song out, and calling one who is near to the one that the crystal is calling for, in this way get in touch with one who is built properly to work with it. For the one who hears the song will report it to his friend, and the friend will hear the song more clearly and comprehend its meaning more fully than the original discoverer. It is not finders-keepers in the world of crystals in this New Age, because energy patterns must agree. You might find a crystal for someone else while they were finding a crystal for you or another.

Once you find your crystal, as long as you are conscientiously learning and growing with the crystal, that crystal will keep its secrets specifically for you. Crystals always work in triads now, for this is the time of the triad energy. One three will join another three making six, then nine, then twelve, yet the generative energy, the point of creation will be in the basic three. In the formations previously, we were working in the Piscean energy, the energy of the two. Now we work in the Aquarian energy, the age of triads. It is well to know this, because when changes take place in the social structure, there is some upheaval and resistance until they are seen as timely, important, and useful.

Allow yourself to feel yourself expanding. Do not get hung up in numbers. See it as a fluid movement. Feel your greater closeness to those about you, and notice that when you meet people now you establish a recognition of their closeness more quickly than you previously have. Notice this and work with it. Hold in the back of your mind, your powerful mind, the thought that you have work to do with each of these beautiful people that you meet and recognize.

Know that within you is a comprehension of what you must do, and that this knowledge will surface as you apply yourself to your own purification. As your consciousness expands, because it has clear, clean space to reach into and fill, you will see more, and into your hands will fall the joyful duties for which you have waited that will bring you to your fulfillment.

◇◇◇◇◇◇

"There is a song in the heart, high tuned and fine, echoing a crystal melody connecting all."

Lesson 33

THE PURIFICATION PROCESS

We see all as beautiful when we see what really is. As we work our way into greater seeing, we pick up elements of untruth that we unwisely design as truth. To rid ourselves of these untruths is our task in the purification process. Often, we get discouraged and see things as more disheartening than they really need to be. There is a process by which we can lift ourselves out of this dangerous self-entrapment. It is a process of instant purification. In it we learn, over a period of time and much practice, to control the emotions with the mind. The creative mind has the power to control all. If we teach it via our emotional control to hold sway in difficult situations, we have overcome one of the most objectionable obstructions to our ability to create purely. You must learn to create purely if you are to work with crystalline energy sources. You can transform your thoughts in a moment and therefore control your speech and actions, if you will it. The mind is a powerful tool, if we use it correctly, with love. Used incorrectly, allowed to build what it will without the discipline of the love response, it builds that which is useless and often distasteful.

Consider formulating a point of power in your mind that will assist you in transforming your emotional thoughts. In that moment when you can go either way—toward beauty and love, or toward disharmony and unkindness—contact this power point, grip it tightly, and exert mental control over your responses. This point of power can be in the form of a poem. We will give you an example. Very simply put, this poem can be powerful, if you choose to make it so. If you are in a situation in which you think you are about to "lose it," if with all your might you are trying to stay high-minded, and it is not working, remove yourself from the source of the problem and say with conviction:

> "I haven't got time to cry,"
>   My voice said aloud
>   As my heart felt the pain,
> "I've got work to do."
>   So into the Universe we explore
>   Leaving behind us no trace of tears.
> Clouds follow us, but *always*
>   We outdistance them
>   Moving with joy above the sorrow.
> To transform one's thoughts at will,
>   *This* is the power of Mind
> And love rides slowly in echoing and answering
>   Every call we cause.

You can write your own poem, if you wish. You can draw on your own resources and create something powerful that will allow you to grab hold of it and lift yourself out of the danger and into the forceful moment of self-mastery of your own mind.

This is one of our greatest tasks. Whatever way we choose to do it, we *must* learn to accomplish this feat above all human will and construct with our minds, our powerful human minds, only that which is pure.

Most people do not like to talk about purification. It makes many people uncomfortable. But you cannot skip this chapter of your life, if you truly desire to work with crystals. The greatest thing that you can do to activate around you that which you desire is to clear yourself. Clearing yourself is an act of purification. As you clear yourself, you will see yourself intuitively stepping out in the right directions to bring that about that will lead to the connections that satisfy your soul urge. There is a long-term pattern of dedication in many, as they work to reveal this plan to themselves, they put themselves through many experiences of purification. At times, this plan gets laid aside. The soul wanders off to take a side trip where he endeavors to find happiness of a self-involved type. Sooner or later, they find it a dead end, and they return to the original path. When one returns with willingness to the sronger pattern, there is always a flooding and a flushing of one's life with new energy. Physical health is usually restored, emotional balance and mental astuteness are regained. One feels a renewed wholesomeness, wholeness to life that had been missed. It is an exciting change.

Frequently, when you take these side trips, you follow patterns that have been unprogrammed, but experienced in other Earth situations, and the calling back of these and the correcting of them are part of the purification process. When you begin to see more clearly, you more easily remember other experiences on the same plane, and you know which former patterns to avoid and which to enhance in your present environment. You set about to use that which would be helpful and are careful to avoid that which would aggravate your true knowing, your clear contact to that which you truly desire. As you expand your horizons, you see more clearly the all that is your soul pattern. You now have the opportunity to rearrange and redesign sectors of other experiences that you might wish to erase or cause to be inert. You now have control over them and can use their power for positive action in the present. Areas in which you found yourself exceedingly helpful and full of love can be brought forward, amplified, and used. Strength in the sinew of the soul structure holds firm as that which can be left behind is abandoned. A greater awareness is moved into with more complete fortification from all worthy parts. Thus does wholeness take place.

In the process of leaving behind that which is not helpful, and moving yourself more into the whole spectrum of helpfulness, you encounter other souls who can be helpful. When you approach the contacts in the spirit of giving and sharing, you can see yourself daily becoming more that which fills your inner need and strongest desire.

In times past, purification was thought to be a task that was best done in aloneness. Not so this time. We are now doing it on a much grander scale than that. Sweeping the whole scope of our memories and contacting all those with whom we have regrets, we clear ourselves of debts and bring ourselves to the golden moment of the present. Binding these contacts into a glorious multiplet, a braid of consciousness, we begin to nourish our whole selves in association with others. We begin to see God in action. We begin to see. Forming out of our past a strong backbone, we hold ourselves more confidently upright. We begin to feel the growth of etheric wings that will transport us whither we wish. It is the path of service.

As you exercise your new purity, you are finding yourself more comfortable with people. Relationships are changing. You are having a broader outlook in your thoughts of contact. You have different and more reasons to start activating an association. You have come through many experiences to bring yourself to where you are now. Use it wisely, this achievement.

When we allow ourselves to leap into our new lives of dedication, we are encouraging many changes. We are saying that we are ready to clear ourselves. This decision sometimes brings on a series of events that to the human eye can look like disasters unforetold. Rest assured they are exactly what we need to bring us into the clearing where we can look about us with a much greater comprehension of what we need to do. It leads us to a clearer view and a greater closeness with others. Most humans hide from each other their most intense moments of regret, but you can understand that those with whom you are drawn into close contact are purifying themselves also. They are going through as intense a program of cleansing as you. Look deep into their eyes, with love, and you will see the same speaking out that you hear calling within yourself.

As we move with these daily works put before us, we will automatically come across those situations that will call for more and more purification.

It will become a matter of course to know that you must and *will* clear out this impediment to get on with the work. The willingness and the effort will be there. The intensification of the interest in the work set before *you* will have the effect of lessening the burden of self-improvement. The mind is stayed on the work and the clearing of your central active soul, and the extended aura becomes a necessary contingent to continuing the work that has caught your heart. Rapidly, the schooling will come through yourself for you to daily participate in the exchanges and interactions which will cause you to draw nearer to your crystal and draw *it* nearer to the surface.

It is together that we learn and together we purify. It is a process that involves many souls coming together and learning kindness. If this seems too simple . . . know it is not. How many times have you thought unkindly? It is not simple. We have work to do.

Remove yourself from the crowd when you must. Design for yourself a place in your center where you can go when you must be alone. Know that you will soon be drawn back into the crowd. You will soon be bumping elbows and exchanging thoughts again, for it is a time of action. The emotions will come to the fore, and you will learn to handle them in a kindly manner. As you do so, you will gravitate towards a more joyful you than you have ever imagined. The being that you are becoming is your expanded self. It has been there all along, but only now do you realize how very marvelously great you are.

⬦⬦⬦⬦⬦

"As we purify, we realize that all is good, all is kindly, and that we are all."

Lesson 34

ONCE AGAIN

Let us once again move back to Atlantis. Sit back. Take a deep breath. Relax and remember. We are climbing some stone steps. Most of us are eight or ten years of age, all male. We are a small group of young students, and our teacher is guiding us through a complex of strange buildings. We are in awe. Most of the buildings have thick walls and no windows. Do you remember? There are flower gardens about, and the wide steps are magnificently carved out of stone. At the head of some of the banisters are gargoylish statues. There are waterfalls and cordoned streams. We can glimpse through the green hedges a tall fountain in a central square which is paved with pink stone. Remember?

Our teacher enters one of the larger buildings. We follow. And as he greets, with an arm clasp, a taller man with a golden band affixed to a portion of his head, we look about in a huge room. Our little faces show excitement as our eyes stare and our jaws open in wonderment. The room seems too large to be a room, yet the walls are entirely covered with a sparkling substance that moves as we look at it like a skyscape at night. It is infinitely more beautiful than anything we have ever seen, and our teacher pretends to not notice our reactions, yet he is carefully calculating each moment to give us proper exposure and impact.

In the center of the room, and he leads us to it now, is a huge machine. It consists of glistening wires and a gold framework around a tube of light which seems to be neither air, fluid, or solid, but all combined. Our teacher's friend climbs aboard the machine, and standing on a silver platform, he reaches his arms high and passes his palms over the white light where it centers itself in the gold frame. A window above on the domed roof opens a little wider as we see the tube of light take form before our eyes and become a thicker mass, a solid crystal. Do you remember?

There was geat beauty in those days . . . and high technology. Are we going back there? No. But we must admire what we did. We can call it again to us, and we can use it. For now, we must be content with our memories and our little crystals buried in the soil where we left them for our return and with our schooling which will lead us to them.

What must you visualize in order to prepare yourself for what you must do when you come upon your crystal? First, know that you are in this day and that you must use what you have now to bring you into the grander scene. Your crystal is lying somewhere pretty much obscured by soil, most likely. It has its own specific abilities and characteristics. During the building process of anything, be it a human physical body or a crystal, there are causes and there are results. Once the structure is built, and it is a complete unit, it has a certain character. It has specific abilities and certain potential. In this respect, crystals are like human beings, there is no end to the variety of structures.

Some crystals are wholly one color. Some are what one might call colorless. The golden crystal, of which we have spoken, is twofold in its color. It has a center of glowing green and an outer crust of gold. There is another crystal nearby that is gold in the center and aquamarine on its surface. It built itself out of its circumstances, and it has certain potential, not unrelated to the golden crystal, but different in purpose, potential, and abilities because of its different structure. They are both gentle, healing crystals. They have formed themselves for the use of imbuing much love and much comfort during the process of healing. The cobalt blue crystal, the one of which we have spoken, is more of a flowing power source. It has the characteristics that will allow it to hold its own as a well of energy which can be dipped into in time of need. As a pool of deep, liquid water, it contains itself more fully than many others, is less of a channel and more of a reservoir in its nature. The red crystal, the ruby, on the other hand, lends itself much more to the generating of earth energy. It will emit constantly and not contain or store. There are some crystals that will serve as generators, some as channels. Some will serve as power sources themselves and draw energy from the depth of the Earth, some will flow with cosmic energy and some will combine the two. Each of them stores in its crystal memory chips much information and power. They all were used in Atlantis during the time of development of the great crystal. So will you call your crystal to you again? And for what purpose? Keep your crystal in mind. Know that you have one with which to serve. Know that it is a healing for you and the planet.

Will there be gardens again as beautiful? Indeed there will! If you will it. And will there be centers of teaching? Can I learn again in an organized and orderly way? Yes, it can be so . . . listen closely to what we have been telling you, school yourselves with it, receive your own memories and proceed . . . with love. The center which builds itself around the energy structures of the blue, golden, and red crystals is already teaching people to work with crystals. As we learn, we teach. We must, each one of us, become students and teachers. It is as this:

> New love I am teaching.
> New love I am learning.
> As I teach,
> I learn.
> I am not infallible.
> I could make mistakes.
> I do
> Yet in me
> Clings a knowing.
> I am learning

And by learning, I teach
    By sharing
What I know, as I learn.
There are those who learn
    Other things than I.
They look ignorant to me
    For I am blind
To what they learn.
    Yet as they learn
They teach,
    Even me
If I am willing.

At this time, there is a certain mystery about it all and that mystery falls into the area of the yet unknown. As we work at our daily tasks following that which we know to be our very highest calling in the moment, we will come clear about one thing. It is this . . . that there is a new world building around us. . . and we are part of it. The more knowledge we can obtain and the more we can act out of kindness, the better prepared we are to assist in this building. Some of the features and facts may seem strange and strain our imagination at times, but we are seeing through a glass darkly. There will come a time soon when we will see more clearly, and the mystery will be that we did not see it sooner. So rest assured that the time of building is at hand and that right now where you are in your present moment is where you are meant to be and that you can proceed from here and all will be well. Let love lead you.

⊲⊳⊲⊳⊲⊳⊲⊳

"Love leads, we follow, creating in pure Light."

Lesson 35

NOW

We can never be assured that the future is to come about as we envision or even as we think we desire. We must best be ready, for our own inner comfort, to be able to go in any direction that God chooses . . . knowing full well that that which is chosen by the Almighty Eye is that which in term becomes the most beautiful. As we progress on the path and interact with the many souls that we call to ourselves daily, weekly, monthly, yearly, then it is best that we be ready to respond to that highest calling, that clearest knowing.

You might ask, "What is to be done now if I am to give the most full love and if I am to be of the greatest service to the most?" The morrow depends on the decisions and actions of many souls. As you respond fully to your call to service, you form no attachments, you yield all to the great unknown. Extend yourself out to others in service constantly. Keep the vehicle, the physical, the mental, the emotional bodies stable, steady, healthy, full of love, and full of Light. Be willing to see what is and to step forward at any moment with what is required of you, if it is in the line of service.

If you do this, you will find yourself developing more understanding of your own abilities and more substantial knowledge of your own calling, that you might establish your own understandable design and workable structure where you will be encompassed about with more of the feeling of home. All things are in upheaval now, for we are in the time before the time of stability.

Within that upheaval, each individual soul can have its own understanding of security when it serves from its center of love. Be content to know that the sun rises each morning, the moon flows with her cool balm nightly and we all revolve in this growth pattern environment on this planet Earth, where we are working toward building a garden exceedingly beautiful and a school that is to be instructive and full of Light. Know that what we build will endure. It *is* worth working for. We are blessed to be chosen, to have chosen ourselves, to work with this most beautiful of creations. What we are sharing, dear friend, is this: *Flower into your greatest consciousness.*

Spend those times in quiet meditation. Be open and receptive to that which is your more free and secure self. Develop yourself until you know that as each minute, each hour, goes by, you have used that time in service and to the *greatest* of your ability. With love for yourself, seeing beauty constantly coming greater and greater from your center, express yourself in love to those with whom you interact each day and do those earth measurements that must be done to keep the physical vehicle healthy.

We move and have our being in oneness. If we would but yield to that which is and see it as beautiful, we would find within ourselves the conditions that would bring about total balance in all our bodies. It is this way in respect to our attitude, also. We see that which we choose to see. In this seeing, we create what we have about us. Each moment we live we are creating our own environment. Are we not creators? We are. In this moment, create that which you would call to you and have as your own. In this moment, design that which would be to the glory of God. You are capable. You are great beyond words, and in this moment you are capable. You are One.

The present is a new creation, an all-seeing moment. All the molecules, the little minerals glowing from the sun, the nourishments that come from the universe to the present moment, vibrate and resonate in you as memories. It is in reality all of the moment, an all-flowering and all-producing beauty. See it as

One. See it as one great moment, sparkling, intricate, full, bursting with glorious Love, bursting with joy fulfilled in the moment. All lives are One. All beings are One. All moments are One. Enjoy!

Alam Selam, go in peace.